D0935451

The regional character of the
Ozarks of Missouri and of
Arkansas is described in this ar-
from the perspective

nt to College and Returned to
Farm." The collection con-
which the few
people live in the

Ozark, Ozark

Ozark, Ozark

A Hillside Reader

Edited by Miller Williams

University of Missouri Press

Columbia & London

1981

Library of Congress Cataloging in Publication Data
Main entry under title:

Ozark, Ozark

   1. American literature—Ozark Mountain region.
2. American literature—20th century. 3. Ozark
Mountains—Literary collections. I. Williams, Miller.
PS556.09   810'.8'097671   80—26242
ISBN 0—8262—0331—0

Acknowledgments on pp. 191–93.

Endless thanks to
Ethel Simpson
Who knew the books I should read
and where to find them
and who interrupted her own good work
many times
with unfailing patience
to point me in the right direction.

Contents

Introduction

We decide, by our politics, where to put the borders of a state. That interplay of land and people we call a region sets its own lines; they are real and permanent, and all we can do is recognize them. Rarely, if ever, have we had the good sense to pattern our states on regional lines, but it has always seemed more important to be from the coast or the plains or the delta or the mountains or the desert than to be from any state. Most people from the hills of Tennessee, I think, would move to the hills of North Carolina before they would settle in Tennessee's flatlands, given the choice. It's the kinds of places we live in that shape our ways, become parts of our days, and form our sense of who and what we are. We belong to a geography and a climate.

This collection is from pens and typewriters in that congruence of land and seasons we call the Ozarks, lying for the most part across the Arkansas-Missouri line, creating a natural community of the relatively few thousand who think of themselves as belonging to those hills, and touching the ways and words of latecomers who have not yet begun to think that. The selections are set down in chronological order, by the birth date of the author, to show something of what happens to the sense of a people moving out of the nineteenth century toward the twenty-first.

It's about a way of talking, a way of coming to know and a way of telling.

The Ozark Mountains are among the oldest geological formations on earth. Four billion years of Time and bad times have worn away at what were never large mountains; their still recognizable culture has not worn away so slowly.

Lola Carolyn Walker, in "Literature of the Ozarks," a 1936 thesis written at Southern Methodist University that still stands as the best review of its subject, suggests that the word *Ozark* (following a pattern in similar borrowings of retaining a preposition and a proper noun) comes from "aux arcs," "to the bows," or "in the hills where good bow wood is abundant."

In the early days, "Ozark" and "Arkansas" were used interchangeably.

The land was French for eighty-three years, from 1682 to 1762 and again from 1800 to 1803, and held by the Spanish for thirty-eight, before it was acquired by the United States as a part of the Louisiana Purchase in 1803. The four decades of Spanish rule had little lasting influence on the culture of the Ozarks. The French influence was of course much greater; at least until the outbreak of World War II there were small towns in Missouri where French habits survived. Walker tells of French festival processions and the New Year's chanting of "La Gaie Anee" in Ste. Genevieve and a patois spoken in Missouri's Washington County. But mostly, distinctly, the culture of the Ozarks has grown from British roots.

The first Americans came into the Ozarks from the Ohio Valley, but most of the early settlers came from Tennessee and Kentucky, descendants of British immigrants from two and three generations earlier. In 1797, Daniel Boone settled at Femme Osage Creek, bringing a large group with him. The town of Franklin, founded in 1816, became the starting point for the Santa Fe Trail, and brought an increasing number of settlers through the Ozarks. Many stayed.

Arkansas was settled more slowly than Missouri, in part because—while the Santa Fe Trail was drawing pioneers through Missouri as early as 1821—Fort Smith did not become the starting place for wagon trails west until the gold rush of 1849.

The Indians were on the land far longer than anyone else, but their contact with the whites was fairly brief, and most often not conducive to the sharing of words and stories. An attack that nearly wiped out the Arkansas town of Natchez in 1730 and a large-scale assault on St. Louis fifty years later were the most publicized instances in a pattern of Osage resistance to the foreign invasion of their homeland, a resistance that ended when the United States persuaded the Indians to sell their land to the federal government and move west. By 1840, hardly any were left in the highlands; little remains to say they were there: a few place names—Cherokee City, Osage, Solgohachia, Hiwasse—arrowheads and potsherds.

Children growing up in the Ozarks never have a thought of the French or Spanish, except in school, and little of the

English. I remember believing—wanting to believe—that every knoll was an Indian burial mound (though these are found farther east and south) and finding arrowheads in plowed fields. But it was the French, who came down from the north, and the Spanish, who came from the south, and the Germans, too, and Italians, who followed the grandchildren and great-grandchildren of the British across Kentucky and Tennessee, who had the greatest part in creating the region as we know it. And so they have made these poems and stories and other writings what they are.

As with most cultures, the first published Ozark writing was non-fiction prose. In 1853 Henry Rowe Schoolcraft wrote a book grandly titled *Scenes and Adventures in the Semi-Alpine Region of the Ozark Mountains of Missouri and Arkansas*. A number of authors contributed to an 1894 collection under the title *A Reminiscent History of the Ozarks Region*, and Charles J. Finger, in 1927, published a widely read book called *Ozark Fantasia*, sections of which are included here. Vance Randolph's popular and authoritative works *The Ozarks* and *Ozark Mountain Folks* were published in 1931 and 1932, respectively, and Wayman Hogue's biographical *Back Yonder* in 1932.

The first poetry of note that I have been able to trace was not published until 1931, when a Boston firm brought out *The Road to Hollister*, 142 pages of blank verse narrative by Ralph Alan McCanse, a story of mountain love lost and found.

Fiction from and about the Ozarks first appeared in 1907, when Harold Bell Wright's *The Shepherd of the Hills* met with great nationwide success. Caroline Stanley told a strikingly realistic story in *The Keeper of the Vineyard* (1913). It was set in Missouri, as were Howard Terry's *A Voice from the Silence* (1914) and William Kennedy's *The Master of Bonne Terre* (1917). The first novel set in Arkansas was Louis Dodge's *Rosy*, published in 1919. *A Daughter of the Ozarks*, by A. M. Haswell (1920) and *Hillbilly*, by Rose Wilder Lane (1926) have us in Missouri, and then *Half-Gods*, by Murray Sheehan (1927) and Charles Morrow Wilson's *Acres of Sky* (1930) put us into the Arkansas hills again.

Sheehan pretends to set *Half-Gods* in Missouri, but it's actually—and obviously—set in Fayetteville, Arkansas, whose citizens took great umbrage at being satirically and sometimes recognizably portrayed.

We're in Missouri again in Louise Platt's *Wild Grape* (1931), set near New Madrid, one of the few towns with a name hearkening back to the Spanish times. It's inhabitants, though, as English-speakers are inclined to do, have moved the accent to the penultimate syllable.

Perhaps the best Ozarks novel of this or any period—and certainly the most accurate picture of the people and their ways, their homes, clothes and speech—was *The Woods Colt*, by Thomas Ross Williamson, a book that was not only a top Harcourt, Brace title in 1933 but did very well as a Bantam paperback as late as 1954. Williamson was so concerned about the authenticity of his story that he got Vance Randolph to read it in manuscript to look for anything that didn't seem right to him. *The Voice of Bugle Ann*, MacKinlay Kantor's 1935 novel about an old Missouri mountain man and his dog, was immensely popular.

1935 is a long way back, but there was no thought of building a complete bibliography into this brief introduction. The titles given (with the much-appreciated assistance of Ms. Walker) are for those who may want to spend time with earlier works, especially the novels that predate the education of many readers. And to say that writing in and about the Ozarks goes back much further than the first dates in this collection.

I would have liked to include selections from some of those novels, particularly *The Woods Colt* and *Half-Gods* and *The Voice of Bugle Ann*, but I was not able to find any sections that seemed able to stand alone. I recommend these books, especially, to any interested reader.

This is one gathering of stories and poems, observations and recollections by which I think the Ozarks might fairly be known. Nothing I can say here would make the changes any more dramatic, nor make the obstinate survival of old turns of phrase, old views and old values more remarkable.

Welcome to the hills.

M. W.
Fayetteville, Ark.
1981

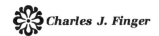 *Charles J. Finger*

from *Ozark Fantasia*

A Joyful River

The other day I saw a new thing, I should say one among the largest of its kind in the world. It was the source of the Roaring River, in the Missouri Ozarks, not far from the town of Cassville. Leaving the regular trail and going by a little road, we came to the giant spring; after rolling through the long, tree-shaded lane. Leaving the lane we were struck by the matchless dignity of a mighty rock precipice, two hundred feet or more high, splendidly adorned with hanging ferns, and crowned by great trees. And going towards that we saw the river, because it is really not a spring, but a river full grown, pouring out of the earth; boiling rather than pouring, for its speed fifty yards from the spring is sixty miles an hour, as it dashes over a high precipice in a marvelous cascade of spraying beauty. The breadth of it is more than sixty feet, its depth more than ten feet. So you may imagine the grandeur of it all in the heart of that dark forest.

Why people who get up road guide books should miss the mention of so fine a corner of the world puzzles me. But no. They will go on with their silly direct advertising, telling about

---

Charles J. Finger was born on Christmas day, 1869, in Willsden, near London. He came to the United States at the turn of the century and settled just outside of Fayetteville, Arkansas, on land still called The Old Finger Place, on Finger Lane. He was a friend of many important writers of his time, who frequently visited him on his own hill in the Ozarks, and he became well known as an author of adventure stories and books. His *Ozark Fantasia*, which was published in 1926 and from which the following selection is taken, was a very popular exploration of the Ozarks as a region of the mind. Finger won the Newbery Medal in 1924 for his *Tales from Silver Lands* and the Longmans Green juvenile fiction prize in 1929 for *Courageous Companions*. At various times he was editor of the magazine *Reedy's Mirror*, managing editor for the Bellows-Reeves Company, and book reviewer for the *New York Herald-Tribune*. He died January 7, 1941.

their banks and their hotels and their garages, as if any of those would attract tourists, and leave quite unmentioned such a natural wonder as this. Sometimes, indeed, the compilers of these guide books act as if they were afraid and suspicious of the joy and beauty of earth. Perhaps that's why they stick up huge advertising boards blotting out some scene of contentment, starting in the light-hearted a mental depression. Indeed, I look upon the impudence of advertisers who deface the landscape exactly as I would look upon the impudence of a manufacturer who posted a man with a megaphone in a concert hall with orders to blare out instructions to Buy Blank's Bathtubs during the playing of the softest passage in Beethoven's Fifth Symphony.

It's the impractability of the man who loves to call himself practical that makes for such stupidities as calling attention to private businesses and leaving out all mention of salient things. No man but will resent the sight of a mustard colored advertisement tacked to a magnificent oak, when he is struck with admiration while passing some clear stream pleasant with large-leaved water-plants. No man riding through flaming autumn woods will be interested to know that the First National Bank of Yodelburg has $30,000 capital. No man thrilled and haunted by the ordered vibrations of a perfect working engine will be cheered by the announcement that Rud's Wrecking Establishment is at Phone 666.

Utopia in Arkansas

Once, I thought that I had found the limit of incongruity. It was years ago, when, on Wellington Island, on the coast of Patagonia, I found on the beach an iron-bound box, and, opening it, discovered a little leather-bound volume, all time-stained and yellowed, and the book was Dryden's *Virgil.* Afterward I went a-sailing with one Bill Potter, a kind of pirate fellow who took up gold-digging, and one day down in Beagle Channel he picked up the Virgil, became interested, and read it with every evidence of vast interest.

But that incident as evidence of incongruity is run pretty close by another of quite recent date, and this later one has a flavor of disjointed ends. It brings to mind Mark Twain's *A Connecticut Yankee at King Arthur's Court*, the swamp city in

Jeffrey's *After London*, or the classic New-Zealander of Macaulay. Idealism and decadence cheek by jowl would be a better way to put it. For once a man named Harvey, prominent in 1896, when sentimentalists and economists were talking about the silver question, made a great deal of money. So, being rich, he set about building a great castle of white stone in the wilds of Arkansas, and the building remains unfinished to this day. There, in a cup of the hills, you see the remains of a vast thing of embrasured towers, of mullioned windows, of arched doorways, and it has the appearance of a feudal castle in process of demolition. To come upon it suddenly, unexpecting any such thing, is like a vision of Melrose Abbey in the Sahara.

The purpose of the man was stranger than his plan, for his idea was that some day,—to put it exact, twenty-five years from 1896,—an ideal commonwealth would be centered about the castle, and the building itself would house poets and philosophers, inventors and philanthropists, scientists and sages, and a golden age would dawn. It was to be a place of the lit lamp and the girt loin, and because of its influence people were to be lifted out of themselves, were to be imbued with high social ideals, were to have a splendid faith in humanity. Above all, the State of Arkansas was to lead her sister States socially, educationally, and morally.

One evening, in the shadow of that unfinished dream of stone, we two who were tramping the hills made our coffee, and while so doing became unpleasantly aware of a boy with a stony expression of countenance who appeared from nowhere and stood watching us, making a very unpleasant kind of noise by whistling through his teeth. He was a lean, fidgeting kind of lad, as ragged as Huckleberry Finn, and he was full of bovine seriousness. Obviously, we had no right to order him off, for he was not interfering, nor was he meddlesome or actively inquisitive. So, in that kindly, authoritative way in which men talk to strange young people of the countryside, we asked him his name. Perhaps he was a dreaming kind of lad and perhaps he was slow of speech, for a long time elapsed before he made reply. Then he said "By-gee," which for a swift moment we imagined to be exclamatory until his head, nodding, showed up our error.

"By-gee," repeated my companion, musingly. Then, "How do you spell it?"

"I don't," he answered very seriously, and added by way of afterthought, "but mebbe my uncle knows how."

We hazarded "Abijah" as a possible solution, but the lad, though mildly interested, was unable to aid us; so there followed a little social catechizing. Could he read? He could a little, but did not. Did he attend school? No; and, anyway, school only "kept" for two months a year where he was, and the last teacher quit because a boy beat him up. What did he do for a living? Well, as to that, he just "got by, like the rest." A little berry-picking, a little wood-cutting, and now and then an odd job. And his spare time, of which he seemed to be so richly endowed, what did he do with that? Well, he "jest hung round with the boys." And at that point we found ourselves in a conversational cul-de-sac. On his part, there were some things he wanted to know. Were we "the law"? If not, why did we go afoot? Had we anything to sell or were we walking on a bet? I think that we left him unconvinced of our lack of ulterior motives, and after a long and searching look at us he turned away.

But, like a figure in a Greek tragedy, he had given us a theme, and as we lay under the stars, in the roofless castle, a host of phantoms arose. For, if this lad was no rare specimen, then indeed he represented a danger, a menace, a wandering fire, and not for nothing had Arkansas at last discovered that she stood forty-sixth among the states in order of educational advantage, that her young men were by the draft test only thirty per cent efficient, that in her public libraries she had only thirty-seven volumes to every thousand inhabitants. And, alas! for Harvey's dream!

The next day we walked many miles without seeing sign of man until we came to a narrow place where the road fell away, so that it was a mere stone ledge in the living rock of the mountain-side, and we had to crowd and make ourselves small to permit the passage of a horse carrying a man, with a woman riding pillion. They gazed at us without speaking, not even answering our salute; but as soon as we were passed, the weather-beaten pair, all grizzled and toil-bent, drew rein to gaze after us. Then at a bend of the road we overtook a man going the same way as we were, and with him we joined company.

He was tall and spare, and seemed careworn, as indeed did almost every one we met on our walk. High on his shoulders he carried a pack covered with a black and shiny cloth. His gray and sparse beard was forked, like the beard of Chaucer's merchant, his shirt was of checkered blue and very irregularly slashed, and it was evident that his trousers had been devised for a much larger man. On his head was a cap such as golf-players use, a head-covering but little suited for a land of beating sunshine. As old as the hills was his sort, and Piers Plowman might have rubbed shoulders with such a one on the Malvern Hills.

For a short while, after a surly greeting on his part, we walked in silence, and we knew that he was filled with that strange suspicion regarding strangers, harbored by the people of the country-side. Moreover, like the lad of the night before and the two on horseback, he looked upon us as curiosities, and it is not nice to be regarded as a curiosity. However, the conversational ice being once broken, we got along very well. His talk was a *macédoine* of tautologies and repetitions, and he had "but smal gramere"; yet from him we learned many things, for he knew the country-side and its people very well indeed. And, let it be said, there was indubitable evidence, when he turned his face to the one or other of us as he said things, that the mountain folk who operated stills harbored no suspicion toward him.

He was, he told us, on occasion a school-teacher, a preacher, a trader in horses and cattle, a berry-picker, and a farmer; and just then he was venturing into new fields, killing two birds with one stone, and following the dual occupation of rubbing doctor and peripatetic barber. His field was, and always had been, limited, for out of the north-western part of the state he had never been, nor did he wish to go. In his own way he had, as Sir Walter Scott said of his Highlander, "all the good manners that nature can teach."

Little by little, as we walked, he unfolded his philosophy, and we learned that in his view the law was a kind of invading entity, the state a sore oppressor. He was, he told us, a practical man and could see no advantage in government. There were no vital connections between him and the state, nor was there a social organism. Instead, each hamlet and village was a compact little realm, each community a separate common-wealth, and there were, metaphorically speaking, stone walls of separation between village and town, between country and city. He was a man most rootedly individualistic.

"Government!" he said with a note of scorn. "Now, look at this town of Red Star. Them there folks pays taxes. If they don't then the gov'ment will sell up a wider's cow or pig. A man'll have mercy. A gov'ment don't know none. And what does Red Star get for it all? Nothin'. Nothin' at all. Protection, says you. But protection 'gainst what, I asks? Police? They don't need 'em. Roads? We ain't got none. Then your gov'ment up in Washington gets into war. What then? Down it comes and takes what it wants. Our men go, and the kids and women folk is left to shift as best they can."

Hearing that, we questioned him somewhat closely, dimly suspecting that somehow he had been touched by Edmund Burke or Prince Peter Kropotkin; but there we were at fault. For understanding presently our suspicion, he very roundly denounced many, naming specifically socialists, anarchists, communists, and prohibitionists, and in comminatory ecstasy bundled with them as objectionable all northerners, foreigners, lawyers, bankers, and especially those who were born in the neighboring state of Oklahoma; for, as it appeared, two from that state had cheated him in a trade, selling him a wry-necked hog. "Every one from Oklahoma," he said, "is tarred with the same stick."

Of the truth of many things that were new and strange to us he was firmly convinced, nor could argument shake him. Thus he revealed to us the curious fact that "the lay of the Milky Way" showed which would be the direction of the prevailing wind for the space of a lunar month; the position of the horns of the moon foretold wet or dry seasons; when there was a ring about the moon, the number of stars within the circle indicated the number of weeks of bad weather; to lay the foundation of a house, to build a fence, to shingle a roof, or to plant potatoes in the dark of the moon was to court certain disaster; in the new house of wood, the resin blisters by spontaneous generation developed into *Cimex lectularius*; a newly born child should be shaken by the heels to the end that its liver should properly fall into place. There was much more of it, and he made the positive statement that the stars and the moon were eternal lamps hung out for signs and seasons, and that the theory of evolution was mere folly.

At noon we came to a place where a group of men were squatted on their heels outside a ramshackle store building. The sorry structure was painted in various colors, red and blue predominating, with here and there, as if laid on by an absent-minded painter, stripes of yellow. On the porch, which was propped up with loose bricks, sat three or four men and a fat woman who chewed snuff, and two yards away a sow and her litter lay sunning.

Our traveling companion disengaged his pack, and busied himself setting out on a sawed-off tree-stump a display of little bottles filled with liquids of various colors, red and blue, green and golden, which, he said were toilet waters and headache tonics. To those on the porch he recounted his experiences as a pain-and-trouble reliever, but his best trade seemed to be in vanilla extract, sold in little flat bottles, for that is by way of being the local substitute for Burgundy. So, seeing him busy, I went into the store to buy some cheese.

At first, in that place, after one had grown accustomed to the darkness, the eye was shocked with the tangle, for there was neither attempt at classification nor apparent desire for order. On a box close to the door slabs of bacon were piled, and a cat with kittens was asleep on a sack thrown over the topmost piece. The shelves were packed with things canned, bottled, tied in bundles, hidden in torn cartons, or stuffed into little chance spaces where they stood or stuck precariously. The filthy counter was littered with a heterogeneous collection: a great cheese, with a wedge cut from it; a dirty pair of scales; a glass case, the top of which was broken, containing a higgledy-piggledy of cheap candy, much fly-specked; part of the carcass of a freshly killed hog, blood-clotted and hideous; an open box of crackers; and, at the farthest end, a little cash-register, with an open Bible atop. The floor was black with ancient filth, and in the middle of it was a stove white powdered with the winter ashes.

A few men and lads were lounging, talking, one telling a story amid an obbligato of remarks. He was foul-mouthed and licentious and malicious. To be sure, he held his tongue a moment or two when a girl came in to exchange eggs for crackers, but she was barely out of earshot before he launched a piece of nastiness that was greeted with squealings. I say squealings, for it was that; not Rabelaisian laughter, but mean squealings, tee-heeings, hyena-like cachinnations.

But, after all, I did not buy the cheese, for just as the storekeeper was about to attend, he was called outside by a man who was lifting a part of a newly butchered hog, evidently the other half of that which lay on the counter, onto a wagon. Having done this service with perfect good humor, he came again to us, ready to weigh out the cheese. But I perceived that he had not washed his hands; wherefore the prospective trade fell through.

We saw, on leaving that place, that our traveling companion was too busy to notice our departure save by the briefest of nods, for he was selling a bottle of greenish hair tonic to a countryman who sought something to cure his wife's headache, and the contents of that bottle the brisk man spiritedly recommended. So we went our way.

Now, as it happens, in the country through which we passed there was much of natural beauty everywhere: richly wooded mountains and sweeping valleys with precipitous sides; narrow roads under expanding roofs of mighty oaks; rutted paths that skirted sheer cliffs; purple mountain masses against turquoise skies and exquisite afterglows of rare sunsets. But what rests in my mind is the memory of men met and of faces seen on the way. There were others we met of whom I might tell, blighted men and women who seemed never to have known youth, but only toil; people lost in solitary wilderness, like the lonely ones of Chaucer. But then, perhaps it were idle to tell more, for the world is full of those who dare not be other than they are.

 *Wayman Hogue*

Our Home Back Yonder

About the first recollection I have of my existence was one day when I was playing in the yard by myself. With a stick I was digging a hole in the ground, when suddenly it occurred to me that there might be danger of digging down to where the Bad Man lived. I had been taught that the Bad Man dwelt down under the ground and that the Good Man lived in the skies.

I jumped up, and looking at the hole I had dug, I thought of how mean the Bad Man had been described to me, and I made a face at the hole, defying him and daring him to come up. I then thought of how powerful the Good Man had been pictured and I made a face at the skies. Thinking over what I had done, I became a little afraid and compromised the matter by saying, "I'll lak ye both if you will let me alone an' not hurt me."

I do not remember the exact house in which I was born, for when I was about two years old my father moved and settled in another county. This was in the northern part of Arkansas, in the Ozark mountains. We were a hundred and ten miles from Little Rock, the state capital, and eighty miles from the nearest railroad.

I had two sisters and a brother, and as I write, a vivid picture of my family rises up in my memory. There is my mother, exacting, commanding, and of a strong determination of mind. My father, friendly, jovial, and always trying to put his best foot forward. Lelia, precise, studious, and refined. Nora, tom-boyish and nervous. Jim, self-assured and executive.

There is nothing I remember more vividly than our old

Wayman Hogue was born in 1870 in Van Buren County, Arkansas, a wild country two days travel from the nearest railroad. After finishing the eight grades of country school, he traveled to school in Little Rock and then taught for several years in schools in Arkansas and Missouri before marrying and moving to Memphis. His first book, *Back Yonder, An Ozark Chronicle*, published in 1931 (in which the following selection is found), was written when he was sixty-two, after he broke a forty-year absence and returned to the Ozarks for a long visit. He died on April 30, 1965.

home and its surroundings. I remember the "big house," one large room built of scalped logs, chinked and daubed, and floored with puncheons made of split logs with the flat side up and the surface hewn smooth. It was roofed with boards riven from choice oak and had overhead joists made of unbarked poles five or six inches in diameter.

There was no loft or ceiling, but some long boards were placed across the joists on which were stored baskets of apples, bags of peanuts and sacks of cotton. I also remember how, in the fall of the year, my mother would slice pumpkins in rings and string them on a stick to dry. These sticks containing rings of pumpkins extending from one joist to another were a familiar sight.

There were two doors in the big house, one on each side, called the front door and the back door. There were no windows, and all light and ventilation came from the open doors and the unceiled cracks in the walls between the logs.

Best of all I remember the huge fireplace at one end of the big house. This fireplace was made of stone quarried from a nearby hillside and cemented together with a mortar made of clay. The extending chimney was built of split sticks heavily daubed and lined with clay, which when dry was very substantial. Sometimes this lining would crack and fall off, leaving the wood parts exposed, and when the weather was cold and the fires large, my father would have to throw water up the chimney to extinguish the blaze.

The doorsteps were made of three sawed blocks which stood on end, one above the other.

I still remember the kitchen, a smaller house of one room that stood out in the yard, facing the back door of the big house, and connected with the big house by a hewn log that was used as a walk from one house to the other.

In the kitchen there was a small fireplace, on the sides of which were skillets and lids, a tea-kettle, a coffee pot, boiling pot, fire shovel, a pair of tongs, and a pair of pothooks, either resting against the walls or hanging suspended from nails or pegs driven into the walls. There was a stationary bench made against the wall on one side of the dining table. The other seats at the table were supplied with chairs brought from the big house at meal times.

The loom, when not in use, stood in the back part of the kitchen, and on it reposed two or three pairs of batting cards.

The coffee mill was fastened to the wall, and the churn occupied space on the hearth near the fireplace.

Against the jambs, strings of red pepper, small bags of garden sage and hands of tobacco were sometimes suspended. Near the door there was a shelf attached to the wall on which rested—in addition to a can of home made lye soap, a jar of salt and a jar of lard—a cedar water bucket with a gourd dipper hanging on a nail just over it. Under the shelf was a barrel containing meal with a meal sack spread over it to keep out the dust.

Just outside the kitchen door and against the wall was a small bench on which there was another cedar water bucket, a tin wash pan, a sardine box filled with lye soap. Hanging over the basin was a towel made from a worn-out meal sack.

The entire family slept in the big house. There were three large cord beds, two in the back part of the house—one in each corner—and the third in a corner next to the fireplace. In place of slats there were ropes running through and around the railings and woven tight. On this network of ropes rested the beds. First there was a straw mattress and on this a full heavy feather bed.

My father and mother slept on one of the beds in the back of the house and my sisters on the other, and Jim and I slept on the bed near the fireplace. We also had a trundle bed under one of the large beds, which could be drawn out and used for company. My mother could always take care of still more company by making down a feather bed in the middle of the floor.

The spinning wheel, when not in use, usually stood by the wall, and there was a large old trunk placed back between the beds, which was used for storing quilts and clothing.

A heavy board was built over the fireplace, which was used as a mantel. On this usually could be seen a large Seth Thomas clock, bottles containing castor oil, turpentine and camphor, and a cake of mutton suet.

Over each door were two forked sticks nailed to the wall with prongs extending outward, called gun racks. A rifle rested on one pair of these gun racks and a shotgun on the other. There was a shot pouch hanging suspended to each of the racks.

We had no rockers and all of our straight backed chairs were bottomed with hickory bark, white oak splits, corn shucks or cowhide.

Our library consisted of a Bible, a small but very thick hymn book, a dream book, a letter writer and an almanac.

The usual way of lighting our house by night was with pine. The heart of the seasoned pine, when split into strips, made a splendid torch, and the knots of decayed pine were very rich in rosin. A pine knot thrown into the fire lighted the whole room. Sometimes, when out of pine knots, we used candles which we molded ourselves. I also remember seeing my mother put sycamore balls in a saucer of grease and light the end of the stem. This made a dim flickering light.

A small rail fence enclosed our yard. It was also well protected by two large and faithful dogs, "Watch" and "Savage." Off by itself in the yard was the smoke house, where meat was hung and smoke-cured.

A short distance from the yard-fence was the barn, usually called the "crib and stable." The lower part of the crib was used for storing corn, and the upper part, called the fodder loft, was used for storing unthreshed oats, fodder and hay. On one side of the crib was a stall in which we housed our horse and mule, and on the other side was a storage for wheat, tobacco, dry hides and baskets of wool.

The crib and stable were surrounded by a heavy rail fence staked and ridered, and we referred to this enclosure as "the lot." Adjoining the lot was the cow pen. We had no shelter for the cattle, sheep and hogs, and they were forced to take the weather as it came.

The outside walls of the crib and stable were often adorned with the skins of wild animals, such as deer, wild cat, and sometimes bear. The walls of the smoke house were ornamented with skins of fur bearing animals such as raccoon, fox, mink and skunk, where my father had tacked them up to dry. The skins of an otter and a beaver, stretched over a board with the pelt side out, were a familiar sight.

Our vegetable garden was on the side of the house opposite the lot, and it was protected by a fence made of long sharp pointed pickets called palings. The palings were pointed at the top to prevent chickens from flying over into the garden, and they were set close together at the bottom to keep out rabbits and fowl.

Our house was built with respect to convenience to water. About a hundred yards from the house was a large spring with a swift outflow from which we obtained our household water.

A few feet from the mouth of the spring was a small excavation through which cold water ran, and in it were placed buckets and jars of milk in order that they might keep cool. They were protected from hogs and cattle by a small rail pen. Near the spring was a large wash kettle and two tubs made by sawing a barrel in halves.

Our field of about thirty or forty acres of cleared land extended down to and included a small creek bottom. In going to the field we passed through the orchard. This was an enclosure of about ten acres independent of the rest of the field.

Our house was situated about a mile from the "big road." This was a rocky, rough, and seldom traveled highway, and was the only road leading out of the vicinity. A creek ran through our property, between our house and the big road, which would often become swollen too deep and swift to ford, and as there was no other way of getting from our house to the big road, we just had to wait until the water subsided.

In describing our old home, I have described the average home of the mountains. It was not much worse and not much better than any other in our neighborhood. It was such a home as my grandfather and my great-grandfather had lived in; we had the same conveniences, the same advantages and disadvantages, as did our ancestors of a hundred years back.

 **Thomas Hart Benton**

America's Yesterday

I had climbed all afternoon a broken, rutted road. As the evening sun dropped out behind the hills, I came to the pass from which the way led down into the valley another twenty miles to the scraped road and the bus line to Little Rock.

On the plateau at the crest of the pass there were two houses and a store. One of the houses was built of logs, in the traditional backwoods style, the other and the store were made of undressed boards nailed vertically to the studdings. All were weatherworn, grey-brown, and, through the warping of the timbers, inclined at precarious looking angles from the stone foundations built up at the corners. Around all were split rail and brush fences.

The store was made of two sections. The front, where a porch hung over the slope, opened on a room with a counter and a few shelves of tinned oysters and salmon. There was a grist mill there and a gas engine to run it. In the back were living quarters, glimpsed through an open door, and off to the side a kitchen with an iron stove which shot its pipe out of the side of the wall. Sitting on the porch was a little boy, teasing a cat with his bare toes.

"Hello," I said, "is this your store?"

"It's Paw's," he replied, looking me over.

"Where is your Paw?"

"He's down in's corn patch. He's hoein'."

"Go tell him there's a man here wants to see him, will you?"

The little boy went off down the hill. I waited in the approaching twilight. From one of the houses came the sound of a melodeon, cracked, wheezy and mournful.

Thomas Hart Benton was born in Neosho, Missouri, in 1889. One of the country's outstanding painters, he was known primarily for his scenes of American life. He studied in Paris as a young man and eventually settled in Kansas City where he headed the department of painting and drawing at the Kansas City Art Institute. "America's Yesterday" first appeared in the July 1934 issue of *Travel*. Benton died on January 19, 1975, in Kansas City, Missouri.

Nearly half an hour passed before the little boy came in sight again, climbing slowly up the hill with his father and mother, their hoes over their shoulders, their feet bare and covered with the red-brown mountain soil. They were young, and the woman was pretty as are so many of the women of hill countries when they are young. As they approached the porch where I was sitting, the mother, without looking in my direction, shied off to the side and ran quickly round to the back, slamming a door briskly as she went in. The boy and his "Paw" came on. I put my business out quickly.

"Friend," I said, "I want to get put up for the night. I've been walking all afternoon and it's too late to make town. Can you give me supper and a bed around here? I can pay."

He reflected a bit. His voice was friendly. "We ain't got no hotel up here. Ah don' know wher' ye can stay. Ah reckon ye can git supper all right but sleepin' over is diffrunt."

"I'm not particular," I said. "I'll be satisfied with whatever I can get. Just a pallet will suit me." Then I explained that I was an artist just bumming around, making drawings of things that interested me. I took my sketch book out of my knapsack and passed it over. The little boy was immensely interested and he and his father went over every page intently. The melodeon kept wheezing and the dark came on without a word between us. I petted the cat.

The little boy spoke up. "Ah like to make pictures," he said.

"Do you?" I replied. "What do you draw?"

"Ah jist makes things up."

"Have you got any of your drawings here?"

"No, we ain't got no paper now."

The atmosphere became friendly. "Well," I said, "don't you think you can find some way of putting me up for tonight?"

"Ah'll talk to the woman," said the man and went indoors.

Time is of little moment in the hills and decision is leisurely, but after a while the couple came out on the porch. The woman, really just a girl, was washed up, her face shiny with soap.

She had on a clean print dress and over her legs that were bare when she came up the hill from the corn patch were drawn a pair of pink silk stockings and on her feet were high-heeled, yellow shoes. She had a straight, clean look out of her wide eyes.

"I reckon," she said, "if ye kin stand we'uns, we kin stand ye."

We had supper and when night had come for good the little boy and his mother took the lamp and went in to bed. After a bit she called out, "All right, Jim," and the man led me into the back room where there were three double beds with high feather mattresses.

"Ye'll sleep in this 'un," he said, pointing to the bed near the door. The boy and his mother were covered up at the other end of the room. "Ah'll sleep here," and he sat down on the middle bed and blew out the light.

After breakfast I went down the hill to the valley. They would accept no pay. In spite of all that has been said about the urbanization and regimentation of American life and the hard inhumanity that goes with it, there remain yet, off the main highways of the country, many areas where character and flavor escape the pattern.

One of these areas is to be found in upper Arkansas in a great triangle extending, with Little Rock as the apex, toward the northeast into the White River country and to the northwest up to where Missouri, Arkansas and Oklahoma join. In this triangle of hill country a belated frontierism persists to this day and people are found whose manners and psychologies antedate those of Andrew Jackson's time. It is a country lending itself readily to romantic interpretation. It has rolling hills, deep valleys, jagged bluffs, rich foliage and clear streams. Set in this background, the log cabin and the rough board house, decked out with the yellow rose and the hollyhock, have an idyllic quality that is persuasive enough to make one believe that here the modern world has failed to put its restless stamp.

The slow language of the people in the back hills and little towns tends again to throw one back into the past and were it not for the sudden interruptions of modern slang, the characteristic English of the neighborhood might readily find a connection with linguistic forms running back into the times of Elizabeth.

But the automobile has come, and with it passable roads and an influx from the modern world bringing its load of new ways, beliefs and habits. These are in the process of being adjusted to the old patterns of behavior and the observing and attentive person can find here the most unexpected attitudes and opinions and contrasts of belief and action that are almost unbelievable. Gross superstitions regarding everything from the immanent presence of Deity to the effect of the moon on the corn crop, side by side and in one mind with the strictly practical and materialistic attitudes of those who handle machines. Immediate, effective and practical actions with plainly predictable results are linked incongruously to hereditary conceptions which belie their significance.

I knew a man, living not far from one of the larger towns in this region, who when he filled the gas tank of his car made a short prayer and called on God to insure the potency of the fluid. And such things are by no means uncommon.

Scattered here and there about the hills are literally dozens of little theological colleges where a most primitive fundamentalism is taught. Among some there persists a belief that instrumental music is an evil in God's sight and this has developed a form of Sunday vocalization without accompaniment of any sort, which is unique in its character. I attended one such "singin'" where even the beat of the foot was tabooed and where the unintended breaks in tune, resulting from the lack of control given by the stamped rhythm, produced the oddest and strangest of effects. This "singin'" was held in a little school house set on the side of a hill under big walnut trees. The men dressed in the standard garb of blue overalls, clean for Sunday, sat on one side of the room, and the women in sunbonnets and straw hats, on the other. The leader stood in the center of the floor and led time with a long, knotty index finger. The hymns I was unfamiliar with, but they were well known to all the participants. There was no preacher and the song was the only form of worship.

The taboo on instrumental music, I found, was the result of the use of the fiddle, banjo and guitar in dancing, which by the seriously religious was regarded as a trap of the Devil. It was profane to bring the Devil's contraptions into the House of God. Nevertheless the leader of the "singin'" sat around home in the evening and played profane tunes on a harmonica for my benefit. The fact that it was Sunday seemed to make no difference as long as he was clear of God's temple.

The towns around the hill country vary considerably in their character but even those on the main arteries of travel, where the garage, the filling station and the soda fountain have found their place, are yet full of the rustic and frequently dilapidated spirit of America's yesterday. The 'seventies, 'eighties, and 'nineties of the middle west manage to survive here. At the county seats, the court house, nearly always of brick, sits in the middle of the square with the false-front frame stores, usually painted white, set round about. The sidewalks, when there are any, are of boards that are sometimes not even nailed down but just laid out for rainy weather. The hitching post is still a factor of importance for the mule is not only the most important piece of agricultural machinery round about, but the commonest means of transportation. On Sundays the squares are full of the oddest combination of vehicles. Automobiles of every variety and description crowd up against wagons, buggies, mules and even sledges which are still used in the roughest part of the hills. There is much heavy timber all about and saw logs and railroad ties are dragged down the hills to the saw mills or roads. I have seen a sledge coming down the hillside with a mule in front and a whole family pulling on ropes attached to the back to keep it from taking a temperamental forward leap which might break the mule's legs.

The hotels, like the towns, vary immensely, and while there are places where steam heat and modern plumbing are to be found, the great majority of hotels in the back hills depend on the old-fashioned pot-bellied stove set in the big front room which serves for the desk and for lounging. The heat gets upstairs as it may. In one back country place the floor boards of the dining room had never been fastened and as the years had warped them, they clattered up and down with every step. The dining room table set in the middle was safe from the worst jogging but nevertheless the biscuits might start bouncing across the table with the entrance of any late arrival. Usually the food in these rustic hotels is all placed on the table at once and you reach for what you want. Late comers are likely to be out of luck and everybody who is going to eat is apt to be found sitting around within easy reach of the call to sit down. Where tourists have entered, and because of the beauty of the countryside and improvement in the roads they are beginning to do so, old-time practices are being modified and instead of the plenty on the big table, lesser portions are set out in the tourist's familiar blue plate. But off the main highways old ways continue and the radishes and the molasses are set side by side, and the long reach controls unabashed the satisfaction of appetite.

The plain people of the hills, like all plain people in lonely places, are hospitable and friendly. Several years ago I attempted a long walk down one of the river valley roads. It was spring and the river was up. The road, like so many in that country, crossed and re-crossed the stream, because of the bluffs of sheer rock which in the winding valley appeared first on one side of the water and then on the other. After several hours of constant fording and re-fording the river with the water mounting higher at each new crossing, I came across one of those charming log houses built by some early settler, which gives so much of the charm of old days to the country. It was in use still and a comfortable place it seemed to be. Cats, chickens and dogs walked in and out of the house, around the big flat stone fireplace and over the floor boards planed smooth with use. In a field at the back the man of the house was ploughing. He stopped work and watched me come up to him.

"Howdy," he says, "wher' ye from?"

I told him where I had come from, the place I was aiming for and asked about the condition of the river fords further down.

"Ye'll never make it," he says. "Ye better turn right round and go back. There's another way of gittin' there but no stranger to these parts 'ud ever find it. Set down and wait awhile an' Ah'll ride ye back."

"No," I said, "I'd like to try this other way. Where is it?"

He looked at me sceptically. "Ye'll git lost easy in these hills," he said. "There's no road, only a trail for a long ways."

I was confident of my ability to follow the directions he would give if I insisted.

"Well," he reflected pointing at the mountain rising abruptly from the end of his field, "the trail goes up thar. Long as ye're on this side Ah can hear ye holler if ye git lost on account of the bluff acrosst the river that sends back the sounds. On the other side the trail gits plainer and if ye git that far Ah reckon ye won't have much trouble. Ah'll take ye part way."

The trail in truth was a difficult one, with the new spring growth hardly discernible, but I made the mountain top and found a plainer road on the other side.

For an hour or so there were no signs of human habitation, only the big timber and the slightly rutted trail. Finally I came abruptly on a split rail fence, some grey-boarded outbuildings and a rambling log house to which additions of all sorts and of all materials had been made from time to time. From a piece of stove pipe sticking out of a leanto smoke was curling.

"Howdy," I called out, "anybody home?"

There was no answer. I called a second time and a third. Finally, like a flash, a woman's sunbonneted head popped out of a glassless window and popped back. Silence and no other signs. I waited a little and then, as if from nowhere, the figure of a man appeared, a rifle across his arm. His big, black hat was pulled down about his forehead and his black eyes and face were devoid of all expression.

There came across my mind suddenly all the tall tales I'd heard about moonshiners and dead strangers who had stumbled into places where they had no business, all the lurid mountain tales with which the town boys had regaled me. I hung my arms across the rail fence to show that I was unarmed. "This road all right for the Gap?" I asked. Through the Gap the road to the county seat passed over the hills.

He pointed with his thumb, saying nothing. I hung on the fence a minute and then turned up the trail. I could feel his eyes in the middle of my back until the foliage hid me.

I have no reason to believe that this man had anything suspicious to hide. Corn whiskey is certainly made in these hills and in considerable quantity but it is not likely that a still would be set near even the least frequented of trails.

There is, beyond the general friendliness and hospitality of the hill people, a strain of taciturnity and suspicion inherited from the hard men who broke the country and for whom a stranger was as often as not a deadly enemy. Once suspicion is around it gets full play and certainly the sudden appearance out of the woods of a total stranger was enough, as in my case, to excite it. The presence of the gun may have been precautionary, or it may have been that the man was simply going out squirrel hunting. In any case, the weapon, the cold expressionless face, the taciturn gesture and the silence of the big timber created in me an uncomfortable feeling that it took a couple of miles of walking to get over.

In the spring or the fall of the year there is no more delightful walking ground in the world than the Arkansas Ozarks. The timber is full, the foliage is rich and the changes in the character of the landscape rapid and varied. As a rule any fifteen or twenty mile walk will put one within reach of quarters for the night.

To a person who is not dressed up like a dude, contacts with the people are easy to make and for the traveling philosopher who would engage in predictions as to the nature of our future social structure, here is a field where he can find what it was before mass production, the movie, the radio and the paved road started it on their present chartless journey.

The future is and must continue to be heavily conditioned by the past and in this land flavored yet by the pioneer spirit, the nature of our fundamental American psychology can be best understood. The people here came for the most part from the Appalachian districts through Tennessee. Mountain born, they stuck to the hills even though the prime impetus for their westward trek was the search for flat lands. Into the valleys the first ones came and the later ones perched on the side of the hills where, as the saying goes, "ye got to prop the corn up to keep it put."

On the journey westward these early settlers of the hills brought with them all the tools and instruments of the backwoods living to which they were accustomed. The rifle, the axe, the two-handed saw, the buck saw, the spinning wheel, the plough and the big, black kettle for scalding hogs, washing clothes and making soap were with every well equipped settler.

On the deeper corners of the hills a sort of pioneer life still goes on, not with the same tools, but in the spirit which their use developed; and the trips to town which all indulge in now, and even the driving of the automobile seem to be not a part of the texture of life but special undertakings similar to the airplane trip for the ordinary urbanized American.

Such expeditions into the ultra-modernity of the movie and the radio as are within the reach of the poor farmer and backwoodsman have as yet only very moderately affected his fundamental psychology. The majority of young people, those growing up since the War, have their feet, of course, on new paths; but even among them there are manifest contradictions between behavior and the pull of inherited beliefs and customs.

Old ways are tenacious and conventions are strong. Dress among the self-respecting males must not be too neat nor must it vary radically from that of their fellows. In the old days clothes were made at home and style was set by very limited powers of invention and execution and ran in a definite groove of uniformity, to which, by necessity, all adhered.

When I was living as a boy in southwest Missouri on the fringe of this Ozark region, men came to town occasionally in clothes of brown homespun, stained, if I remember rightly, with a dye got from the outer shell of walnuts. But the day for such home industries as dyeing and weaving is now past and today the overalls, the blue shirt and black slouch hat form the standard male garb. The overalls are frequently stuffed down into short boots but the comforts of home, particularly in summer, call for bare feet and many a husky will be found on Saturday afternoons in town, sitting in his wagon bed, easing his feet for a while between excursions around the stores.

The boys of the towns, of course, wear the conventional Chicago suit. They go without coats in the summer and their arm garters, keeping their shirt sleeves up, run like their suspenders towards as much gaiety as possible. The town boys are not as friendly as their back country cousins and a stranger has no easy time getting in with them. They have their cliques and their manners and are likely to be suspicious of the pretensions of an outsider.

In the towns, especially in the county seats, on a Saturday night one runs across surprising numbers of the old-fashioned drummer. The mail order houses and the big manufacturing firms have not altogether knocked out the old methods here and the loquacious, slick-tongued salesman with his bags and stories yet finds a field where the personal touch is worth more than the quality or desirability of goods. Some of these drummers are really traders in the true sense. I knew and traveled with one who, in a rickety car to the rear of which a great box-like cupboard was bolted, made the rounds of all the little settlements and isolated stores of the back country and traded a cheap grade of coffee, and three-for-a-penny candies, for ginseng root and picked walnuts. Wherever a car could go, he worked his trade, dickering for long hours, telling stories and making himself at home with and a part of the life of the people.

Ginseng root, which grows wild in the half-shady places of the woods, is assiduously cultivated. When a man stumbles across a patch he erects a canopy of dried branches over it so that the sun just flickers through. Experience calculates the right amount of shade and sun. A good crop is profitable. The Chinese use ginseng in great quantities as a part of their medicinal concoctions and through that little root even the lowliest hillbilly of Arkansas can, with a little luck, find himself a factor in the stream of international trade.

Another feature of the past still surviving in the county seats of this region is the medicine show. With a tent and a rough stage and a couple of blackface minstrels, these shows, providing a rough and ready music and a run of broad and simple jokes into which the element of sex enters only where the old maid is concerned, can draw every farmer and family for miles around. Ten by fourteen posters, stuck on the telephone poles, advertize the advent of Dr. Soandso's famous show and the sale of his miraculous medicines. The doctor puts on his big performances always on Saturday afternoons and evenings when the towns are sure to be full of people. He mixes his entertainment judiciously with the exposition of the qualities of his medicines, and while he is talking his entertainers work the audience standing in a packed mass before his tent. Fifty cents for relief, a dollar for a sure cure.

> "Ole black Sam, he rode down thar
> To buy his mule a new cigar."

The banjos fall to at just the rightly calculated second before the crowd grows restless under sales pressure. The tricks of holding and selling are developed here to a degree of neatness and precision that is utterly disarming, and the bottles and packages find plenty of buyers before a session is over. What rheumatic old man or woman can resist the pull of hope?

I asked one of the town druggists what he thought of these shows. "Well," he said, "those medicines don't hurt anyone. They don't do much good, I guess, but they draw the people to town and while they're here they buy from the rest of us. I always do a good business when one of these shows is around. Once the people get the idea they need something for their ills, they don't quit with the show's stuff but shop around a little and we can sell them reputable goods. All the storekeepers around feel that they're a pretty good thing for trade."

Traditions and the old ways fight still the entrance of the modern world in this country but in a little while they will break down and the very last of our father's America will be gone.

 *Otto Ernest Rayburn*

I Arrive in the Hill Country

My mind itched with expectancy during my first night in the Ozarks. I slept lightly. I was up with the dawn, threw cold water into my face from the porcelain bowl, supplied by a large pitcher on the dresser, and came down from the hotel to find the town spring cutting a dido for my entertainment. It had a rock and roll that fascinated me. I had no wax in my ears and the music of the tumbling water was a Siren's call that captured my fancy. The recent heavy rains had swelled the volume of the spring that normally flowed a million gallons a day. The village of Reeds Spring, a thriving trade center of Stone County, Missouri, was built around this mammoth spring.

I had arrived in the village the day before by way of the White River Division of the Missouri Pacific Railway. I did not come to the Ozarks as Opie Read entered Arkansas in the 1880's, counting the ties as he walked toward Carlisle to join his companion in setting up a print-shop and starting a newspaper in a box car. I rode the cushions in style, changing trains at Aurora, that smug little city that once wanted to be the capital of the United States, diving into the hills all steamed up for adventure. I had an excellent supper at the hotel, served family style, with an attractive waitress at my elbow, and

---

Otto Ernest Rayburn was born May 6, 1891, on a farm near Bloomfield, Iowa. He traveled in his youth to New York, London, and Paris, decided early that he didn't care for city life, and returned to the small towns of Arkansas and Missouri. He became one of the most important writers and speakers on Ozark folkways. After serving with the U.S. Army in World War I, he taught school in Arkansas, Missouri, Kansas, and Texas, published two volumes of poetry (*The Inward Real*, 1927, and *Dream Dust*, 1934) and several books of observations on the Ozarks, and edited *Ozark Guide Magazine*. "I Arrive in the Hill Country" was first published in *Forty Years in the Ozarks* (1957). He lived his last years in Eureka Springs, Arkansas, and died in 1960.

retired early. It rained a little during the night as April passed out and May moved in.

That big spring tumbling from the bowels of the earth in the center of the crazy-quilt town! A million gallons or more of crystal clear water each twenty-four hours! It was one of the first large springs I had seen and my eyes were as big as a giant's pocket watch. I picked up a tin cup and drank to my fill. It is an old tradition that if you take three drinks from an Ozark spring you will always return for more. I drank and became an adopted Ozarker. Looking at the village, lighted by the rising sun, I was captivated. I never before had seen such a storybook town outside the pages of a book. It fired my imagination. The stores and shops were set cattywampus around the spring, defying all the rules of the architect. It was a square that had not been squared. It had an individualistic appeal and I liked it. From all appearances each man had built his house as he blamed pleased. It was absurd from a mathematical point of view, but who cares about geometry in the Ozarks. There are no straight lines in the hills. The circle predominates. Ralph Waldo Emerson said: "The eye is the first circle; the horizon which it forms is the second; and throughout nature this primitive picture is repeated without end. It is the highest emblem in the cipher of the world." Reeds Spring was shaped like an old bicycle tire squashed out of shape. Emerson would have considered it a crude emblem in the world's cipher. The hotel was set on the hillside at a rakish angle, a hop and a jump above the spring. The houses of trade would have been apropos to Alice's Wonderland. It was fantastic to me, a lubber from the level land. It threw my head into a tail-spin.

Reeds Spring rubbed its eyes early that May-day morning and, as the sun rose, women came to the spring for water for the breakfast coffee. They gave me no mind except a sly look from the corner of an eye. Had H. L. Mencken, the iconoclast, been with me at the spring, he could have read hard lines in their unsmiling faces and stamped them with his disapproval. With him, much of the behavior of mankind was a jumble of contradictions. He enjoyed giving everybody hell. He once visited the Ozarks and his comment in the *Baltimore Evening Sun* of January 19, 1931 is a sour classic of frankness, fringed with insult. He wrote:

Several years ago I enjoyed the somewhat depressing plea-sure of making a tour of the country lying along the border between Arkansas and Oklahoma. I can only say that I came out of it feeling like a man emerging from a region devastated by war. Such shabby and flea-bitten villages I had never seen before, or such dreadful people. Some of the former were so barbaric that they didn't even have regular streets; the houses, such as they were, were plumped down anywhere, and at any angle. As for the inhabitants, it is a sober fact that I saw women by the roadside with their children between their knees, picking lice like mother monkeys in the zoo. The fields were bare and the woods were half burned. There were few fences. When one appeared, usually far gone in decay, there was always a sign on it, painted crudely with the e's backwards PREPARE TO MEET THY GOD.

Charles Angoff in his biography, *H. L. Mencken: A Portrait from Memory*, says that the famous writer had poor literary taste, but I don't know about that. It is true that he was an image breaker and did not mince words in his ridicule.

Reeds Spring did not have what you would call regular streets and the houses were "plumped down anywhere," but the town did not appear flea-bitten and shabby. It was individualistic. It was original. The women I saw did not belong in Mencken's category.

At the present time (1957) Reeds Spring has a modern look. The town has been dressed up and has become a thriving trade center for southern Stone County. Being a gateway to the new Table Rock Lake, it has a bright future. Not many of the earmarks of 1917 remain today.

Breakfast at the hotel was a delight. The waitress was coy, but friendly. I ate half an orange as a starter, then ham and eggs with hot biscuits. I drank two cups of Arbuckle's coffee. I feasted like a harvest hand turned epicure.

After breakfast, I circled a herd of hogs that were rooting in the street, and made my way to the real estate office that hung on the brow of the hill where the business section dips into the holler. The proprietor had a big chew of tobacco in his jaw and a ten gallon hat on his head and was ready for business. He was a strange looking fellow with a long chin and ears that reached almost to the top of his head. A bad sign in the marts of trade, but I didn't believe in signs. I introduced myself and told him I was looking for a small tract of land, preferably near a good fishing stream. He studied for a minute or two, scratching his long chin with his trigger finger. He began marking on a piece of paper on his desk, probably making up a bill of sale in his mind at the same time. "I believe I have just what you want," he said. The marks on the paper began to look like the map of Stone County. "Follow the Old Wilderness Road south twelve miles to Kimberling's Ferry on White River. About a quarter mile from the ferry is a forty acre tract covered with cedar and oak and other trees. It has a partially built log cabin on it. No water, except a wet weather spring, but there is a good all-year spring on adjoining property at the foot of the hill. The price is $200. If you go down, stop at the Henry Thomas place. Mr. Thomas will show you this land."

This description appealed to me and I made preparations for the trek to White River. I left my baggage at the hotel, went to a grocery where a friendly moon-faced merchant sold me cheese and crackers for lunch. At ten o'clock I started down the Old Wilderness Road. It was the first day of May of that fateful year of 1917. The hills were fabulously dressed in coats of many colors. The dogwood was in full bloom and a few redbud remained to give a pleasing background of color. The solid forest lay in green folds in all directions with an occasional clearing that showed a log cabin and signs of life. This was a road for lingering, but I had twelve miles to go and kept walking. Once I stopped to talk with a farmer who was cultivating corn on the side of a hill. He rested his mule when we exchanged greetings. No soil could be seen, but there was corn peeping up between the rocks. The hillman explained that these rocks were a real help to the farmer. They kept down weeds and preserved the moisture. I couldn't understand how corn could grow in such soil, but I was a novice and had much to learn about the Ozarks.

Passing Yocum Pond, the halfway point, I entered a scenic wonderland that held me enchanted. The wrinkled earth with its sun-jeweled canopy of sky appeared to me as a picture I had seen, but this was the real thing. A line of fog showed the course of White River, meandering through the hills. In the dim, distant blue, hugging the horizon, lay a range of hills which I knew to be Arkansas, and somewhere in that layer lay "Carcossonne," which I would know, years later, as Eureka Springs, the "Switzerland of America."

After drinking from this overflowing cup of inspiration, I returned to earth and sat on a rock by the roadside to eat my lunch of cheese and crackers. Then I started the descent into

"Utopia," following the trail toward the river. An hour later, I arrived at the home of Henry Thomas, made arrangements for the night's lodging, tried fishing in the river without success, then sat down to a good supper with the Thomas family. They set a good table of homegrown vittles. No fatback or sow bosom with redeye gravy. In my *Ozark Country*, written twenty-three years later, I fictionized this meal as follows:

Supper with this Ozark family made an indelible impression in my mind. I had arrived, an unexpected guest, an hour or two before mealtime, but there was no scarcity of food, no framed apologies. The table was loaded with good things to eat. Crisp bacon was served with delicious crackling corn bread. There was yellow butter from which the moisture had all been "whacked out" with a cedar paddle. Baked beans, brown and savory, were dished from a blue crock. A pitcher of cold buttermilk from the springhouse sat alongside a platter of lettuce, radishes and onions from the garden. There was fluffy wheat bread, baked at home, with apple jelly if one cared for it. For dessert we had ginger cake and dried peaches that had simmered in their syrup through the long afternoon. To partake of such wholesome food in such a pleasant environment was to slip back in imagination to the Elizabethan age of old England. These folks belonged to an aristocracy of brains and honor with a pedigree that isolation does not weaken. Later I came to know many such old-line families in the backhill country of the Ozarks.

I had heard it rumored that Ozark cooking was not fit to eat and that the hillman's face was framed with a hungry look that hinted of gastric incompetence. This meal convinced me that these rumors were false. In the tall corn country of Iowa we lived on the fat of the land, and on the Kansas prairies we feasted abundantly, but these prosperous regions of the level land did not have a thing on the Ozarks. I was convinced that the crudeness of the hillbilly is largely a fable cooked up by literary artists to entertain. Of course, there are exceptions and I discovered some of them later, but this did not alter the high rating I gave the Thomas family.

The hillman of the Ozarks is cousin to the ridge runner of Kentucky, the swamp angel of Louisiana, and the sod buster of Kansas. They all live close to the earth and are branches of the same tree. These people produce men worthy the name and we look to them for deeds of heroism in times of war. Alvin

York was a Tennessee ridge runner; Audie Murphy, a Texas sod buster.

Supper over, I sat in front of the fireplace with Mr. Thomas, locally known as "Uncle Henry," and his two grown sons, Bill and Bud. The boys rolled cigarettes made from Bull Durham tobacco. The grown daughters, Nova and Sally, washed the dishes in the kitchen. We talked about fishing and farming, and discussed the war which our country had entered less than a month before. The evening passed too rapidly to suit me. I had found an Anglo-Saxon seed-bed in the fat marrow land of the Ozarks and was reluctant to leave it. But hillfolks do not keep late hours, and at nine o'clock Bill took a lamp and lighted me to my room. I sank into a bed of feathers and immediately went to sleep.

The next morning I took a look at the "forty" and it was "love at first sight." It would be my haven from the restless world. I recalled Emerson's statement: "He who knows what sweets and virtues are in the ground, the waters, the plants, the heavens, and how to come at these enchantments, is the rich and royal man." This spot would be my workshop and exercising ground. It would give me an opportunity to know nature and copy her ways. It was a visionary concept and quite impractical, but I was carried away by it. The reality of bread and butter was forgotten. Later on I learned the hard way that bread and butter is an item quite necessary to the good life.

Bill Thomas was driving to town and I rode with him in his jolt-wagon to the branch road that led to Marvel Cave and the Shepherd of the Hills Country. Bill told me that he was the mail carrier in Wright's story. I was anxious to see this fabulous Mutton Hollow country with my own eyes. Footloose and fancy free I followed the compass of my inclination. I walked toward the land where Harold Bell Wright had found himself a dozen years earlier. Within an hour I approached the little store and post office at Notch where Levi Morrill, the "Uncle Ike" of *The Shepherd of the Hills*, was merchant and postmaster. The old man gave me a cordial welcome when he found out that I was from Kansas. Mr. Morrill had been a newspaper publisher in the Sunflower state and his brother had been governor.

After a short chat with "Uncle Ike" and a look at his store and post office, I crossed the road to the home of Henry Lynch and his two daughters, Miriam and Genevieve. The Lynches owned Marvel Cave, reputed to be the third largest cavern in the nation, and I wanted to see it. I broke bread with this family who were Canadians by birth and Ozarkers by adoption. The food was delicious and the serving had a Victorian elegance that gave the family a high rating in my esteem. This was the beginning of a friendship that has lasted forty years.

Dinner over, Mr. Lynch took me to the cave a short distance down the valley. I visited this cave many times in the years that followed and at one time acted as an emergency guide for a day or two, but this first visit with Henry Lynch as guide made an impression that I have never lost. Mr. Lynch was a man of character and vast learning; a gentleman and a scholar. He was in love with his cave. I have never met a man so obsessed with passion for a material object. The beauty of this vast subterranean cathedral of nature has become a part of his life. This put a stamp on his personality that set him apart from other men. We talked as we walked and I learned how this man of culture had come into possession of the cave; how he had developed it; how it obsessed him. I was sold on Marvel Cave even before I entered it.

We descended into the cavern by a long ladder to the top of a huge mound of earth called "Pike's Peak." At this point we lighted candles and followed the winding path to the floor of the vast cathedral room which is one of the finest examples of cave architecture to be found anywhere. I tried throwing a rock across the room, but it fell short of its mark. The acoustics were perfect. The sound waves of a whisper went to the far reaches of the room. I saw the Liberty Bell stalagmite, said to be the largest formation of its kind in the world, drank from the spring called "the Fountain of Youth," and then started the winding descent through the bowels of the earth. The squeeze through "Fat Man's Misery" and the crawl through "Bill Sunday's Knee Drill" were exciting. About five hundred feet down we reached a tumbling waterfall that beggars description. It is "honey in the rock" so far as subterranean scenery is concerned.

I spent two hours in the cave with Mr. Lynch, but we visited only a small part of it. Many miles of passageways have been explored in this vast cavern, but not all of them are open to the tourist public. The trip to "No Name River" through the "Giant Crevasse" is a hazardous journey and only trained spelunkers attempt it. I once started this trip, but met a convoy of bats in a narrow crevice and they almost smothered me. I turned back. The cave is the home of millions of bats and Mr. Lynch pointed out numerous clusters of the little creatures clinging to the ceiling.

Many improvements have been made in Marvel Cave in recent years by the Hershend family who now operate it. Electric lights and improved walks make it a comparatively easy trip. An elevator is now being installed to eliminate the long climb out of the cavern.

In mid-afternoon I bade farewell to Mr. Lynch and started walking toward Branson, eight miles away. I followed the trail "that is, nobody knows how old," and passed the little cemetery which is the final resting place of some of the leading characters of Wright's story: Mr. and Mrs. J. K. Ross (Old Matt and Aunt Molly), Mr. Levi Morrill (Uncle Ike), and Mr. Truman Powell (the Shepherd). I paused to look at Old Matt's Cabin on the north rim of Mutton Hollow, then followed the trail over Dewey Bald to Jim Lane's Cabin at the foot of the mountain. From this point it was an hour's walk to Branson.

It was corn-planting time a dozen years earlier when the stranger of Wright's story followed the Old Trail into the Mutton Hollow neighborhood and lodged with the Matthews. Within this brief period the tale had become legend and tourists were flocking in. It was another twelve years, however, before the trail was made suitable for motor traffic. In 1929, I bumped over it in a Model-T Ford. This trail is now a part of a paved thoroughfare—U. S. Highway 148.

Arriving at the resort town of Branson on White River (Lake Taneycomo) I put up for the night at the Branson Hotel. The next morning I explored the town, took a look at the lake, and then boarded the noon train for Reeds Spring to close the land deal and pick up my baggage.

I now belonged to the aristocracy of land owners and the thought gave me much satisfaction.

A flashback is necessary at this point of my story to correlate certain facts that appear to be contradictory. In 1909-10, I attended the academy of Marionville College, a Methodist school at Marionville, Missouri, without realizing that I was in the Ozarks. This little town is in a well-developed farming region and not much different from the Kansas country I knew. The Ozarks seemed to be a place remote; a strange land of song and story, like a fabled Utopia. I had a wonderful time at the academy and was awed at the wisdom of my teachers, especially Dr. William H. Howard, who taught mathematics, but I did not get the feel of the hills. I was treading in academic water and my interest, at the moment, was education. It required a special stimulant a few years later to arouse an interest in folklore and folkways. This came when I read *The Shepherd of the Hills* about 1916. Folklore and the Ozarks seemed to be tied up together. I had never thought of Iowa or Kansas as having any folklore although I grew up waist deep in superstition and was nurtured on a primitive religious concept. I was a part of the folk but did not know it. I am deeply indebted to Harold Bell Wright for the stimulation he gave me. He opened my eyes. Without him I might have missed the Ozarks entirely. It is strange what a book can do.

 *Vance Randolph*

Verbal Modesty in the Ozarks

One of the most interesting peculiarities of the Ozark hill-man's speech is the extraordinary character of his conversational taboos—the singular nature of his verbal reactions to sexual and skatalogical matters. The truth is that sex is very rarely mentioned save in ribaldry, and is therefore excluded from all polite conversation between men and women. Moreover, this taboo is extended to include a great many words which have no real connection with sex, and which are used quite freely in more enlightened sections of the United States. The same general principle applies in the Southern Appalachians, and perhaps in other parts of the Southern hinterland, but the examples in this paper are those which I have heard myself in the Ozark Mountains of southwest Missouri and northwestern Arkansas.

In general, it may be said that the names of male animals must not be mentioned when women are present—such words as *bull, boar, buck, ram, jack* and *stallion* are absolutely

Vance Randolph was born in Pittsburg, Kansas, February 23, 1892. At twenty-two he graduated from what is now Pittsburg State University and went on to take a masters degree in Psychology from Clark University in Worcester, Massachusetts. After a time in New York, where he lived in Greenwich Village and found work as an editor and ghost writer and published a poem in *The Masses*, he returned to Pittsburg to teach in the high school and write for a socialist weekly newspaper published in Girard, Kansas. He served in the infantry and artillery in World War I, and returned to settle in Pineville, Missouri, where—after a flirtation with studying for a Ph.D. in psychology at the University of Kansas—he became seriously involved in the study of folklore. He worked with Alan Lomax collecting folk songs, was elected first president of the Arkansas Folklore Society (after moving to Eureka Springs in 1947), received an honorary doctorate from the University of Arkansas, became a Fellow of the American Folklore Society, and published the large number of articles and books that have established him as the major figure in Ozark folklore. He died in Fayetteville, Arkansas, November 1, 1980.

taboo. Some writers[1] think that *buck*, meaning a male goat or deer, is not generally objectionable, but I cannot agree with them. It is a strange thing, however, that *Buck* is quite admissible when used as a man's given name, and in this connection may be pronounced freely by men and women alike. The same thing is true of such compound substantives as *buck-shot*, *buck-ague*, *buck-brush*, and *buck-skin*.

De Vere[2] says that many Southerners use *ox*, *male-cow*, or even *gentleman-cow* instead of the English word *bull*, but the Ozarkers in my neighborhood usually say *male*, *cow-critter*, or *cow-brute*. It was only a few years ago that two women in Scott County, Arkansas, raised a great clamor for the arrest of a man who had mentioned a *bull-calf* in their presence. Even such words as *bull-frog*, *bull-fiddle* and *bull-snake* must be used with considerable caution, and a preacher at Pineville, Missouri, recently told his flock that Pharoah's daughter found the infant Moses in the *flags* — he didn't like to say bull-rushes! It is generally supposed that these absurd euphemisms are no longer prevalent among civilized Americans, but *male-cow* appeared in an American scientific journal as late as 1917.[3] The hillman sometimes refers to animals merely as the *he* or the *she*, and I have heard grown men use such childish terms as *girl-birds* and *boy-birds*.

A stallion is sometimes called a *stable-horse* and very rarely a *stone-horse*,[4] the latter term being considered unfit for respectable feminine ears. Such words as *stud* and *stud-horse* are quite out of the question, and a tourist's casual reference to *shirt-studs* once caused considerable embarrassment to some very estimable hill-women of my acquaintance. The male members of most species of domestic animals are designated simply as *males*. *Cow*, *mare*, *sow*, *doe*, and *ewe* are used freely enough; but *bitch* is taboo, since this last term is often applied to loose women. *Whore-bitch* is a common Ozark term for prostitute. To call a hill woman a *heifer* is to call her a meddlesome gossip, and a *sow* is simply a slatternly housekeeper; but neither term has any particular sexual or moral significance.

The male fowl is usually called a *crower* — the word *cock* is quite out of the question, since it is used to designate the

1. Taylor, Jay L. B. Snake County Talk, *Dialect Notes*, Vol. V, part 6, 1923, p. 214.

2. De Vere, Schele. *Americanisms*, New York, 1872, p. 488.

3. *Journal American Medical Association*, Nov. 17, 1917, p. 24.

4. Clapin, Sylva. *A New Dictionary of Americanisms*, New York, 1902, p. 387.

genitals. One writer[5] reports that *chicken-cock* is common in southeastern Missouri, but it is very rare in the Ozarks that I know. Farmer[6] defines *crower* as "a prudish euphemism for cock" and adds that this is not the only instance in which the Americans "fall from the frying-pan of squeamishness into the fire of indelicate suggestiveness." The word *rooster* is also used as a substitute for cock, and Farmer characterizes this term as "the product of an absurd mock-modesty." De Vere[7] quotes Dr. Hugh Clark to the effect that "*rooster* is an American ladyism for cock," and an anonymous Englishman who swears that Americans often say *rooster-and-ox* when they mean cock-and-bull! I have myself seen grown men, when women were present, blush and stammer at the mere mention of such commonplace bits of hardware as *stop-cocks* or *pet-cocks*, and avoid describing a gun as *cocked* by some clumsy circumlocution, such as *she's ready t' go* or *th' hammer's back*. Such expressions as *I roostered my ol' hawg-leg* are not at all uncommon in this latter connection, and when a hillman says *I pulled back both roosters* he means only that he cocked both barrels of his shotgun. The word *peacock* is very bad, since it is supposed to suggest micturation as well as the genitalia. Even *cock-eyed*, *cock-sure* and *coxcomb* are considered too suggestive for general conversation, and many natives shy at such surnames as *Cox*, *Leacock*, *Hitchcock* and the like.

Many mountain women never use the word *stone*—the commoner term is rock, anyway. De Vere[8] has observed the same reluctance in other parts of the South, and refers to "a young lady who was so refined that she avoided saying *stone*." He does not tell us just why this term is considered objectionable, but I fancy it is because *stone* is sometimes used to mean testicle, as in the compound *stone-horse*, which means stallion. This usage is found in the King James version of the Bible,[9] a work with which most of the mountain people are more or less familiar.

The Ozarker very seldom uses such words as *virgin* or *maiden*, since these terms carry a too direct reference to sex. A

5. Crumb, D. S. The Dialect of Southeastern Missouri, *Dialect Notes*, Vol. II, part 5, 1903, p. 309.
6. Farmer, John S. *Americanisms Old and New*, London, 1889, p. 186.
7. De Vere, Schele. *Americanisms*, New York, 1872, p. 381.
8. Ibid., p. 554.
9. *Deuteronomy*, 23, 1.

teacher of botany tells me that he is actually afraid to mention the *maidenhair* fern in his high-school classes. *Decent* is used to describe women who have no sexual experience outside of lawful wedlock, but the term is not used in polite conversation between the sexes. "Fifty years ago," writes H. L. Mencken,[10] "the word *decent* was indecent in the South; no respectable woman was supposed to have any notion of the difference between decent and indecent." *Decent* is still indecent in the Ozarks. *Ravish* and *ravage* always mean rape in the hill country, and are not mentioned in polite conversation. Even the word *bed* is seldom used before strangers, and the Ozark women do not *go to bed*—they *lay down*.

There are no crabs in the Ozarks, but the word *crab* is used to designate a tiny pest which the entomologists know as *Pediculus pubis*. Since this parasite is usually confined to the areas about the sex organs the name of it has acquired an indecent connotation. The tourist may talk of shrimps and prawns and lobsters without let or hindrance, but the first mention of *crabs* is greeted by an awkward silence, or by embarrassed efforts to change the subject.

Even the apparently innocent verb *alter* is never used in the presence of women, because *alter* in the Ozarks means to castrate, and is never used in any other sense. *Rim* means to desire sexual intercourse, and is applied particularly to swine—never used in general talk between the sexes. *Stag*, meaning a gentleman who appears at a social function unaccompanied by a lady, is a new word brought into the country by tourists—the natives regard it as vulgar. *Cagey* and *horny* are the ordinary words for sensual, and are never used in polite conversation. *Balled-up*, according to Mencken[11] was once improper, but is now making steady progress toward polite acceptance. This is doubtless true in the more sophisticated sections of the country, but *balled-up* is still bad taste in the Ozarks.

A paper bag is always a *sack* or a *poke*, since *bag* means scrotum in the hill country, and is too vulgar for refined ears. It is said that *bag* has the same indecent connotation in certain parts of Kansas.[12] The sex organs in general are frequently known as the *prides*, and the word *pride* has thus acquired a

10. Mencken, H. L. *The American Language*, New York, 1921, p. 152.
11. Ibid., p. 176.
12. Ibid., p. 152.

certain obscene significance. When a hillman says that he *got him a piece* he means that he has had sexual intercourse, and thus an intrinsically harmless term like *piece* has become unfit for refined society in the mountains, and must be used with considerable caution. The word *parts*, too, is so often used to mean genitals that it is no longer decent in the Ozarks.

When the word *ill* is applied to a woman it usually means that she is bad-tempered, but sometimes it refers to menstruation, and *unwell* is always used in this sense—a man or boy could never be described as *unwell* in the Ozarks. The individual who is afflicted with a serious disease is neither ill nor unwell, but *sick*. The term *flowers* is also used with reference to catamenia; Dr. Morris Fishbein[13] has noted this, and regards it as a modern slang term. It is found in Webster's New International, however, and in the King James version of the Bible.[14]

Another doubtful word is the proper name *Peter*. This is so universally used by children and facetious adults as a name for the penis that it never quite loses this significance. Very few natives of the Ozarks will consider naming a boy *Peter*. I recall an itinerant evangelist from the North who shouted out something about the church being founded upon *Peter*—he was puzzled by the flushed cheeks of the young women, and the ill-suppressed amusement of the ungodly. Another preacher, a real Ozark circuit-rider, after talking about Peter's denial of Christ, suddenly called out: *How many Peters air they hyar?* There was no laughter or snickering about it—the people were simply horrified, and the poor preacher almost collapsed when he realized what he had said. This happened almost thirty years ago, but it is still remembered and commented on whenever this preacher's name is mentioned. *Petered out* means simply exhausted, and has no particular connection with sex, but I have several times noticed that a native stumbles and hesitates over this phrase in the presence of strangers, particularly women. He feels somehow that it is just a trifle off color—not quite the thing to say *right out before folks*.

Pregnancy is another thing which is never mentioned when both men and women are present, even among fairly intimate friends. If no women are within hearing, a hillman may remark

13. *American Speech*, October 1925, p. 24.
14. *Leviticus*, 15: 24, 33.

to a comparative stranger that his wife is *ketched*, or *knocked up*, or *in a family way*, but these phrases are not for use in mixed company. A pregnant woman is expected to stay at home and keep out of sight as much as possible, never intimating to any man except her husband that she has the least inkling of her own condition. The word *slink* must be avoided, too, because it means to abort or to miscarry. A midwife is always called a *granny-woman*, and *granny* is often used as a verb, designating the actual delivery of the child. It is sometimes employed with reference to the lower animals, and I have heard a hillman speak of *grannyin'* a cow. These terms are never used in general conversation between the sexes. Even *birth-marks* are mentioned and passed over hurriedly—never described or discussed.

Many of the hill people still shy at the word *leg*, and usually say limb, particularly if the speaker is a woman, or if the member under discussion is feminine. Farmer[15] has discussed this matter at some length, but the general idea is that since women's legs are concealed by their garments they should not be exposed in speech. The younger women no longer conceal their legs, but something of the old taboo still lingers in the common speech; legs are to be seen, perhaps, but should not be talked about. *Stockings*, too, as Clapin[16] points out, are considered rather indelicate—one always says *hose*. Something of the same sort has occurred in connection with *breast*, and the word *bosom*, which is not common in ordinary American conversation, is still the proper term in the Ozarks.

Even *love* is considered more or less indecent, and the mountain people very seldom use the term in its ordinary sense, but nearly always with some degrading or jocular connotation. If a hillman does admit that he *loved* a woman he means only that he caressed and embraced her—and he usually says that he *loved her up*. Such terms as *passion* and *passionate* are never used save in connection with sexual desire, and must be avoided in polite conversation. The hillman sometimes eats sheep's testicles, which he calls *mountain oysters*, but these are believed to contain a powerful aphrodisiac, and must not be mentioned when ladies are

15. Farmer, John S. *Americanisms Old and New*, London, 1889, p. 346.
16. Clapin, Sylva, *A New Dictionary of Americanisms*, New York, 1902, p. 234.

present. No modest mountain woman would ever admit publicly that she is fond of eggs, because eggs also are supposed to excite sexual desire. The word *tail* is frowned upon for some reason or other; Carr[17] tells us that *shirt-tail parade* is regarded as indelicate even at the University of Arkansas, *nightshirt parade* being considered much more refined!

The noun *ass* must be avoided because it sounds exactly like the Southern pronunciation of *arse*,[18] and even *aster* is sometimes considered suggestive. A variety of elm tree which carries a large amount of sap is known as the *piss-ellum*,[19] but needless to say this is never mentioned in polite Ozark conversation. I have seen one of our solid citizens painfully embarrassed because he inadvertently said *manure* in talking with a mountain schoolmarm, and sly allusions to this devastating *faux pas* followed the poor devil for years. A casual mention of the game called *hockey* will paralyze any Ozark audience, for *hockey* means nothing but dung in the hill country. Any mention of laxative drugs is considered in very bad taste, and I shall never forget the country druggist who was horrified when I called for Pluto water while he was selling candy to some young girls. I remember also a grown-up mountain woman, the mother of several children, who blushed scarlet when she heard *physics* mentioned as a part of the high-school curriculum. Modest Ozark women never say *urine*, but use the word *chamber-lye*, even when talking to a physician.

The word *bastard* must not be used in ordinary talk, of course, but *woodscolt*, which means exactly the same thing, is not prohibited. A woman who would be highly insulted if the word *bull* was used in her presence will employ *Gawd-amighty* and *Jesus Christ* freely as expletives; these words are not regarded as profane, and are used by the most staunch Christians in the backwoods districts. Women of the very best families *give tittie* to their babes in public, even in church, without the slightest embarrassment. Such inelegant terms as *spit* and *belch* are used freely by the hill women everywhere, and I have heard the wife of a prominent professional man tell her daughter to *git a rag an' snot thet young-un* — meaning to wipe away the mucous matter from the child's nose. On

17. Carr, J. W. *Dialect Notes*, Vol. III, part 1, 1905, p. 94.
18. Bach, R. M. *Vulgarisms and Other Errors in Speech*, Phil., 1869, p. 34.
19. Taylor, Jay L. B. *Dialect Notes*, Vol. V, part 6, 1923, p. 206.

another occasion she remarked to a total stranger that her husband had *done got drunk ag'in an' plum benastied hisse'f*. This same woman would never use such words as *leg* and *breast* in the presence of strange *men-folks*, and would blush to hear of *gonorrhea* or *syphilis*.

So much for prudery in the Ozark dialect. Perhaps a century or so of isolation is responsible for an abnormal development of this sort of thing, or it may be that the mountain people have simply retained a pecksniffian attitude once common to the whole country. But these questions must be left to the scientific students of dialect. The present influx of tourists and summer-resort people is rapidly wiping out the old folk-speech—a few more years and the hill people will be talking just like the rest of us. Meanwhile, it is probably worth while to record such data as are now available, to be mulled over later by the lexicographers.

Literary Words in the Ozarks

One feature of the Ozark dialect which has often impressed me, and which has not been mentioned in any of the previous papers on the subject, is the frequency with which some illiterate hillbilly brings out perfectly good English words of a type very seldom used by illiterates in other parts of the United States.

Where else, for example, would one hear an unlettered woodcutter use the verb *cavil*, as in the sentence: *Them fool women is allus a-cavillin' 'bout somethin'?* Not in New England certainly, nor in the Middle West, nor anywhere in America except the isolated hill regions of the Ozarks and the Southern Appalachians. I was amused when the principal of a high-school, a graduate of Missouri University, told me that *cavil* is "hill-billy slang, not good English at all."

A mountain woman once told me that her husband was *mighty dilatory 'bout writin' letters*. I afterwards discovered that neither of them could read or write, and how the woman came by such a word as *dilatory* is still a puzzle to me. Another neighbor was very fond of the word *proffer* — *th' ol' woman she proffered fer t' git me a bait o' vittles*. The verb *partake* is very commonly used, even in the most isolated communities. I recall one man who remarked: *I don't never partake of no whiskey 'cept if I'm a-ailin'*. This same fellow told me that he had never seen a locomotive, but he had seen plenty of airplanes — a strange thing, when one stops to think of it. . . . It was this man's son, I think, who described his wife as a *docile critter*, pronouncing *docile* with both vowels long, and no noticeable accent on either syllable.

One often hears the word *bemean*, as in the sentence: *I hates a feller what's allus a-bemeanin' of his kin-folks*. The word *forsake*, too, is in common use among the hillmen, who speak of a girl as *forsaken*, meaning that she has no suitors. The good English word *fray*, meaning a fight with deadly weapons, is still common in the Ozark country; so is the noun *jaunt*, although usually pronounced so as to rhyme with *rant*. The noun *caucus* is unknown to the hillman, but the verb forms are not unusual, in such sentences as: *th' women-folks is a-caucussin' 'roun' somers*.

An old woman once told me of a song-ballad her little boy had copied into a friendship book: *Jim he wrote hit off fer me, an' th' schoolmarm she rectified hit* —meaning that she corrected a few errors in spelling and punctuation. This boy, by the way, was described as *a apt scholar*. One of my neighbors is often spoken of as a *plum contentious woman*; a man remarked to me that *thet 'ar wind shore denotes rain*, adding that he hoped it would *cease* before morning. I once heard an illiterate moonshiner ask indignantly: *You-all reckon I caint discern right from wrong?* —the word *discern* did not seem to fit his mouth, somehow.

Just the other day, in Pineville, Missouri, I heard a woman say: *Hit's a plum tragedy fer me t' eat sparrergrass*, and the word *tragical* is often used in similar sentences. The verb *creen* signifies to lean or to twist slowly sidewise, and is evidently an abbreviated form of *careen* —a word seldom used by farmers or woodsmen in other parts of America. The verb *beguile* is not at all uncommon. A little boy remarked to me that *ol' man Landers he don't play at no dances nowadays—jes' fiddles roun' t' beguile th' time*.

One of my friends, convalescing from a serious illness, was said to *meander* around, a reference to his slow and wavering gait; a flashily dressed young photographer was warned not to *delude* any of the local virgins; the Baptist preacher is known as one who *comprehends* booklearning, and is able to *clarify* the most difficult and ambiguous passages in the Bible. The word *oracle* is used in a peculiar fashion: *whutever th' ol' woman says is th' oracle in this here shanty, an' don't you never fergit hit!* The verb *wrest* is unusual in the ordinary American illiterate's vocabulary, but the Ozark hillman often uses it in such sentences as: *I was that weak, Doc, I couldn't wrest a tater off'n a baby!*

The Ozarker seldom *thinks* about any serious subject, but prefers to *study* or even to *ponder*; the adverbs *candidly* and *actually* are often heard in his ordinary conversation, while *wearisome* (with the first two syllables pronounced *wary*) is not at all uncommon. The noun *onset* means a fight, and one may speak of a *master onset* between two dogs in the street. The verb *pen*, meaning to write, is often heard among the older people, and I have heard *penned* used as an adjective.

I have noted many other words which impressed me in the talk of these illiterate hillmen, such as *loiter, peruse, with-*

stand, genteel, betide, agile, honorable, reconcile, exhort, dote, intoxicate, diligent, and *generate*.

All of these words, of course, may be found in the average college graduate's vocabulary, although I have my doubts about some of them. But they certainly do not occur in the speech of ordinary American workmen in most parts of the United States, and the fact that they *are* used by these illiterate Ozark hill-people is therefore worthy of note.

A Good Song Well Sang

My respectable neighbors all warned me to keep away from the "scrapin's o' th' woods" who lived on Tedlock Knob, but it seemed to me that the Tedlocks were not particularly bad people—just ignorant, and shiftless, and ornery. And this, remember, was before I discovered that they were my kinsmen.

They didn't own any land, but merely squatted on this barren hillside which belonged to some "furrin" capitalist. None of them had ever been known to "work out" for anybody in the Holler, and they never had any crop to sell—just raised a little corn and garden-truck for their own use. They were hunters and trappers and fishermen, and made a little money by digging ginseng and golden-seal in season.

There were four families in the Tedlock clan, and four tiny cabins perched on a limestone shelf some hundred feet above a spring on the rocky hillside. It would have been just as easy to have built the cabins close by the spring, or at least on a level with it, but that is not the hillbilly way of doing things.

"Th' men picks out th' place for th' house," one old woman told me, "an' they don't keer how fur off th' spring is. They know it's allus th' women-folks whut has got t' tote th' water."

And so it was that the Tedlock women had clambered up and down between the cabins and the spring until their bare feet had worn a path deep into the rugged side of Tedlock Knob.

The menfolk seldom came into town more than three or four times a year, while the women never showed themselves in the settlement at all. They never got any mail, never went to church, never attended any of the neighborhood social gatherings. There were no legal marriages among them, either, but the Knob swarmed with children of all ages. The Moon Valley school was not more than a couple of miles away, but only three or four of the Tedlock youngsters had ever attended it. The teacher at this place was a friend of mine, however, and it was through her that I first became acquainted with the "scrapin's o' th' woods".

This schoolmarm was much interested in my collection of Ozark folk-songs, and had already given me several very fine old ballads obtained from her pupils or their parents. One evening she told me that the Tedlocks had a very ancient "family ballet" which they refused to sing or even discuss before any outsider. Little Annie Tedlock, she added, had been severely punished just for telling her that such a song existed!

Because of the popular feeling against the Tedlocks it was not practicable for the schoolmarm to visit them. It might displease the school directors, she said, and she was a little afraid of the big boys over there, anyway. She suggested, however, that since I had neither job nor virginity to lose it might be well for *me* to cultivate the outcasts of Tedlock Knob, and try to get the secret "ballet".

Well, I hunted and fished and drank with these people for several weeks, usually with Peyton Tedlock, who seemed to be the most approachable and enlightened member of the clan. Extreme poverty is nothing new to me, God knows, but I was certainly a little shocked the first time I visited Peyt's cabin. Dirt floor, no windows, no light except that from the open fire—these things are common in the back hills. But never before had I seen a regularly occupied home which didn't have any beds. Peyt and his family slept on piles of leaves and straw, with a few tattered quilts and comforters thrown over them.

Peyt's wife brought me a new tin pan of clean water, and after I had washed my hands she rinsed the pan and used it to mix her cornbread in. While the bread was cooking on a greased johnny-board before the fire, she washed the pan again, and fried a piece of fat pork in it. A few minutes later the pan was scrubbed out once more, and served as a coffeepot. After the meal I suppose she washed the dishes in the pan, too. It was the only sizeable cooking utensil she had, and she seemed to be very proud of it.

The Tedlocks knew that I was collecting old-time songs, and we all sang a while after supper. I wrote down the words of several of Peyt's old favorites, and told him of others which I had obtained from local singers, but was unable to draw out any reference to the family ballad.

Several days later I came right out and asked Peyt about the Tedlock song. He admitted that there was such a piece, but was horrified at the idea of singing it for me.

"Ye see, Vance," he said apologetically, "that 'ar ballet is plumb different t' these hyar common songs. Hit brings good luck an' keeps off evil sperrits, an' all like that. My fore-parents fetched it acrost th' water way back yander, an' thar ain't nobody in th' world knows it only th' Tedlocks an' their kinfolks. I give Annie a lickin' jest for namin' it t' th' schoolmarm! Naw, sir, if I was t' sing you that 'ar song th' charm'd be broke, an' th' Tedlock family 'd be ruint forever!"

As I looked about Peyt's miserable shanty I couldn't help wondering just what the word "ruin" could mean, as applied to these poor creatures. Sickness, I suppose, and death; certainly they had no worldly valuables to lose. However, there was nothing more to be said on the subject, and I definitely gave up all hope of ever adding the Tedlock ballad to my collection.

And so it was that I did not climb the Knob very often that Winter, and the dogwoods were in full blossom before I ever met old Granny Tedlock, the real head and oracle of the clan. The old woman's eyes were dim with age, but her mind was active enough.

"Yas, I've heerd considerable 'bout you," she said, as she put her skinny old claw into my hand. Then she peered at me in silence for a long minute.

"Whar' bouts did your folks come from?" she asked finally.

"Virginia, then Kentucky, then Tennessee," I told her, adding that I myself was born in Kansas.

"Whar 'bouts in Tennessee?"

I named several towns in the eastern part of the state.

After some further questions about the names and various migrations of my forefathers, the old woman said sharply: "Whut did your folks call theirselves, back in Tennessee?"

"Randolph," said I.

"Jest plain Randolph, eh?"

"Well, some of them used the name Fitz-Randolph, I think."

Granny Tedlock grinned. "You know whut that 'ar *Fitz* means, don't ye?"

I nodded, and the old woman cackled shrilly.

"He's a Randolph, all right," she told the rest of the family. "His Pappy must of been one o' ol' Tom's boys. I hearn tell how Tom went t' Kansas. *Him an' Peyt thar is fourth cousins!*"

The sudden acquisition of these new and disreputable relatives "sot me back right smart", but I grinned as cheerfully as possible under the circumstances. Cousin Peyt and I took several whacking big drinks by way of celebration, and on my next visit I brought Granny Tedlock a gaudy woolen bathrobe, which seemed to please her very much.

Several days later it suddenly occurred to me that since I was, in a measure, a member of the Tedlock clan, there was no longer any reason why I should not hear the Tedlock ballad. When I said as much to Cousin Peyt he hastened to consult Granny about the matter, and after some family wrangling it was decided that I was now entitled to hear the song.

Cousin Peyt looked about outside to make sure that there were no cowans or eavesdroppers in the vicinity. Then he cleared his throat and assumed a singularly dignified expression. Like a priest at the altar, or something of the sort. I was impressed in spite of myself. His gaze on the distant hilltops, Peyt took up his song in a wild but strangely pleasing fashion:

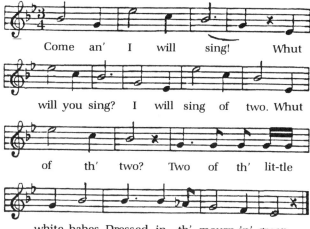

Come an' I will sing! Whut
will you sing? I will sing of two. Whut
of th' two? Two of th' lit-tle
white babes Dressed in th' mourn-in' green.

Come an' I will sing!
Whut will you sing?
I will sing of three.
Whut of the three?
Three of them was strangers,
Two of th' little white babes,
Dressed in th' mournin' green.

And so the weird chant went on, in dreary but somehow impressive repetition, with one additional line for each new verse. There were eleven of them altogether, and here is the final stanza:

Come an' I will sing!
Whut will you sing?
I will sing of twelve.
Whut of th' twelve?
Twelve of th' twelve apostles,
Eleven of th' saints that has gone to Heaven,
Ten of th' ten commandments,
Nine of th' sunshine bright an' fair,
Eight of th' eight arch-angels,
Seven of th' seven stars in th' sky,
Six of th' cheerful waiters,
Five of th' ferrymen in th' boat,
Four of th' gospel preachers,
Three of them was strangers,
Two of th' little white babes
Dressed in th' mournin' green.

"A good song well sang!" cried old Granny Tedlock, and I added my voice to the general chorus of approbation. I recognized the piece as a degenerate variant of the so-called *Dilly Song*, which was sung a long time ago in England. The original was used in traffic with supernatural beings of a decidedly non-Christian character, and the less said of it the better. Probably there are not many people in America who know anything about these matters nowadays, except a few students of balladry and the like.

Cousin Peyt sat down and wiped his forehead with a dirty red handkerchief.

"Whutever you do, Vance," he said solemnly, "don't *never* sing that 'ar song t' nobody outside o' th' family. Us Tedlocks is a-doin' purty good hyar lately"—his gaze wandered to the shining tin basin hanging on the wall—"an' I wouldn't have th' charm broke for nothin'!"

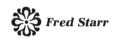 *Fred Starr*

The New Calf

Today we had a blessed event on our farm. The old roan cow gave us a fine heifer calf.

At milking time she was missing. With a cloud coming up, I went in search of her and found the two on the hill back of the barn. They were hidden in a clump of scrub oak bushes and underneath the protecting branches of a large cedar. Strange how sensible like even a cow can act at birthing time.

The mother was calmly giving her new offspring a bath with her long, rough tongue as it stood on wobbly legs.

A lot of queer sayings and still queerer superstitions about cows abound in these hills.

When hill folks want to let you know a thing must be done over they say, "You'll have to lick your calf over."

They say of a hill's steepness, "It is steep as a cow's face."

Getting their mind made up about a thing, they stay with it until the "cows come home."

Having recently lost a valuable cow and wanting the mother and her baby to do well, I'm trying to remember and follow the advice of all the neighbors.

I'll remember to use a bucket for the first milk although it ain't fitten to use, because to milk it on the ground would cause the cow to go dry.

I'll wean the calf when the signs are right to keep it from bawling its head off. I'll not kill any toad-frogs for fear old Roan will give bloody milk. I'll breed her when the moon is right so's to have another heifer calf at the blessed event next year. But I'll be hanged if I'm going to stay up on Christmas Eve until midnight to see whether the new calf has learned to kneel and worship or not.

Fred Starr was born in 1896 in Waco, Georgia, and made his way to the Ozarks about 1925. He was for some years an educator in the schools of Arkansas and Oklahoma and served in the Arkansas General Assembly from 1955 to 1959. He wrote several books of essays, observations, and recollections about the Ozarks, and authored weekly columns for the *Tulsa World* and the *Northwest Arkansas Times*. He died in November 1973.

Setting a Spell

It's porch-sittin' time here in the hills and no hour of the day quite compares to it.

The chores are done. Supper is over. The milk has been carried out to the spring house. The birds have found shelter for the night, all save the troubled whip-poor-will, who pours out his haunting call from the hill above the house.

The sun has bedded down for the night and twilight reaches its long, slender fingers—first into the hollows—finally touching the distant hills. From across the river comes the cry of hounds on a warm fox trail. A mockingbird rouses and decides to practice a few musical notes. The faint tinkle of a cow bell eases through the heavy quietness as old Brindle lies doddling her head and placidly chewing her cud.

A neighbor drops in for a chat.

"No, don't bother 'bout bringin' no cheer. I'll just set here on the porch floor an' lean agin a post. Ain't got much time nohow."

"Well, what's your hurry? Did you come after a chunk of fire?"

There is choice bits of news about a new baby in a family that has all too many mouths to feed already. There was wedding last Sunday and the death of an old man yon side the mountain this morning.

The hour grows late. "Hit's purt nigh 9 o'clock."

The neighbor says good night and is swallowed up by the darkness. The whip-poor-will has grown tired of complaining, the fox hounds have lost the trail.

There is the scraping of chairs. "Better take ever' thing in. Hit's liable to rain a-fore mornin'."

The hillman has reached the end of a long busy day and falls asleep by the time he hit the bed to be up with the sun.

No aspirins, no headaches, no hangovers. He leads the simple life. Is it any wonder he has to kill a dog to start a graveyard?

Omens

To jump a stream, springing from the left foot and landing on the right, is bad luck. The curse may be removed by running around a tree three times, closing your eyes, counting seven and jumping back across the water flat-footed.

In carrying a baby across a stream better see that its head's turned up the creek or else it's shore to die by drowning.

Washing your hands in stump water will prevent warts.

Stranger things than either truth or fiction happen hereabouts. A visitor from across yon mountain has just departed leaving the following story behind.

It seems he moved from an east Texas oil field a year ago, and he still wonders at the strange ways and customs of his neighbors; so different from those in the the country from which he hailed.

Last spring the old man in the family nearest him fell ill. Wanting to be a good neighbor the former Texan started going over each night to set up. In fact he was there when the old man and father shuffled off this mortal coil and passed over the river in search of much needed rest.

The newcomer was not so upset about the procedure in the presence of death. He had an inkling from others what might happen should the old man die. He had been told there would be the stopping of the clock to ward off bad luck. In fact, he rather expected the clock to stop of its own accord when the old man died. The mirror was covered taking precaution against some one seeing themselves in it and being the next to go.

But strangest of all to this stranger in this land: When he returned next morning to go about helping bury the dead, he found the oldest boy out in the orchard among the bees. It seemed he had torn long, narrow strips of black cloth into a sort of crape and had these streamers hanging before each hive.

For a while he stood and watched this strange ceremony. The son going from hive to hive, knocking on each and apparently muttering to himself. Finally he asked of the boy the why of his doing. The son looked at him in astonishment and said,

"Why I'm telling the bees about paw's going away. It is swarming time and if I don't tell them they might leave while he is still here and that would be bad luck. It would mean another death in the family right soon.

"And not only that, but it might mean bad luck for the whole neighborhood. Why, one time paw's cousin died and nobody told the bees. They swarmed and one of his boys was killed going back to Kansas from the funeral."

Remedies

We were discussing various home remedies for this and that, and he claimed sich had saved more lives than doctors. Not bein' in a argufyin' humor an' knowin' well an' good tryin' to convince a hillman agin his will you'll git nowhere quick for your troubles, cause he'll be of the same opinion still—he's that much like a woman—I give him mine and absquandered some of his'n.

Sassfras leaves carried in the pocket often relieves the worse case of galling. Not the kind where a feller what owes you an' owes you comes a-borrowin'.

Take nine sups of water—very slowly—to cure the worst case of hiccoughs. Wetting on a heated fire shovel will dispose of a kernel in the groins in short order. A dime in the roof of the mouth will stop nose bleed. Wearing the same dime or an old bullet on a string around the neck will keep the nose bleed from getting a head start.

Going to the crossroads and saying, "Sty, sty, leave my eye, catch the next one passing by," will remove a sty if the moon is right and the chantin' is done nigh on to sundown.

Holding a burn close to the flame will draw the heat out and help to relieve the ailing member. Lard and vinegar or kerosene—maybe you say coal oil—will break up a cold. Spider webs and soot will stop bleeding of a wound. A pan of water under the bed will stop night sweats and a double-bitted ax placed by the pan of water will cut the worse pains. Grease a rusty nail no sooner than it is pulled from the youngen's foot and he will not have tetanus. Tallow melted with turpentine and applied to fresh wounds will also prevent blood poisoning.

 *Leonard Hall*

Four Seasons at Possum Trot Farm
from *An Ozark Journal*

Sumacs Are Blazing and Geese Fly Low

One evening last week I landed home in a driving rain and hurried into boots and old clothes to get the chores done. It was cool enough for a wood fire so there were logs to be carried in for the fireplace, as well as the chickens to be fed and shut up for the night. The old girls had been out in the rain all day and if there's anything more bedraggled than a wet hen, I'd like to see it. I shooed them into the henhouse and hoped they wouldn't catch their death! Then up the hill to the wood-pile. The rain slackened, along about that time, and clouds in the west began to thin out and let the sunlight through. A rainbow suddenly spanned the eastern sky and then a second one appeared above the first. Within a moment the whole countryside was filled with a translucent golden light and the western horizon burst into flaming, blazing color.

I called to Mama who quickly donned her boots and we hurried to the hilltop to catch the full glory of that sunset. There was a strong wind blowing, driving before it the birds which were homeward bound. A pair of doves and then another drove by like small rockets, veering sharply skyward to dodge the electric wires along the road. An old blue heron, making slow headway, beat laboriously down our valley toward his roosting place by the river. A flight of grackles

Leonard Hall was born in Seneca, Missouri, in 1899. After service in World War I, college, and twenty years in business, Hall moved to Possum Trot Farm near his Ozark boyhood home, where he lives today with his wife, Ginnie. Here his *St. Louis Post-Dispatch* and *Globe-Democrat* columns, his books, and his wildlife films have brought him national note as naturalist, defender of wilderness, and rustic philosopher. Four of his columns from *Country Year: An Ozark Journal* (1949) are reprinted here.

drifted along like leaves blowing and two nighthawks, so low that their wing bars showed sharply, complained as they were buffeted about.

*   *   *

The sun dropped below the clouds and made a red ball on the horizon's rim. In the single moment before it was gone, colors in the valley and along the river and out across the far hills were all etched in a hundred variations. Each tree took on its own distinct and individual green, from the silver-gray-green of the willows by the creek, to the yellow-green of hickories on the hill, to the clear, pale green of hard maples nearby, to the solid black of the far-distant oaks across the river. Then the sun was gone and the colors fused together and no longer stood out in sharp contrast, though the western sky blazed brighter.

Across this blaze of color swept a black band of clouds hard-driven by the wind. They came up out of the west, and then, as though meeting a strong cross-wind, swung sharp to the north like a troop of marching men. A thin scud of mist came racing up out of the south, the rainbow faded and the big drops came slanting down again and drove us home to the fire. Deep in the thorn trees, as we came down the hill, we could hear our mockingbirds complaining in soft whispers about such outrageous weather. But that sunset had been a fine thing to see. Later, when I went for more logs for the fire, it had cleared again. A huge moon was coming up and, in the woods across the river, the big owls were hunting.

*   *   *

It's hard to say whether we're glad to see autumn come or not. After a long season of gardening and canning it isn't bad to look forward to a time of leisure. But then there are so many things we'd like to get done before bad weather closes down that we aren't quite sure about it. This morning we couldn't put off any longer the fact that autumn has arrived. As I came up from the chicken yard I heard it. I looked down toward the river and, sure enough, there came a line of geese. They were flying low and with slow wing beat and honking disconsolately as they came. Then the long V lifted sharply to clear our hill and we watched them disappear slowly into the sunrise. Soon they'd hit the Mississippi and turn south again on their journey.

*   *   *

Next morning, heading up the road for town, I realized how summer had stolen away from us. Many of the trees, it is true, have taken advantage of recent rains and stayed green. But the hickories have turned yellow and leaves are floating down from the walnut trees. Sassafras and sumac are blazing along the fence rows. The goldenrod, bright yellow a week ago, is starting to fade and soon the honey harvest will be ended. Over along the edge of the field, the deep red foliage of the dogwoods shows in a pattern of horizontal layers and here and there the tip of a sugar maple is turning scarlet. The persimmon trees have lost many of their leaves so that the bright fruit and grotesque black branches stand out like a Chinese painting against the sky.

The bright orange-red bittersweet is ripe, now, and fruit on the haw trees is turning from dusty pink to frosty blue. The wild grapes made a big crop this year and we had meant to pick some for jelly, but that's another of the jobs which will have to wait for some future and less strenuous year. It's good, though, with a sharp tangy taste which makes it ideal for serving with game.

*   *   *

As a matter of fact, there are lots of odds and ends of autumn harvesting still to be done. We have quite a crop of peanuts which must be dug and hung to dry before roasting. We don't know of just what quality these will be, but I'm sure the birds and squirrels will like them when winter arrives. There are also a few sunflower heads to be harvested and saved for the winter songbirds. And the last of the green tomatoes gathered for pickling—and the rest of the late potatoes to be dug.

*   *   *

Last week we started harvesting honey and the first "super" came off the hive with a total of only two bee stings! I wouldn't have gotten those if I'd remembered to tie up my pants legs. Maybe I was a little too rough in brushing the bees from the honeycomb as each well-filled frame was lifted from the hive. At any rate, I brushed them off into the long grass behind the hive and it isn't surprising that, with several hundred bees crawling around in the grass, a couple should find their way up my trouser leg. We've still got several more supers to empty of their honey and after that will get the hives ready for winter. And now I see George heading down the hill to cut corn and it's time I was off to the city.

*   *   *

Folks from Vermont like to talk about their cold weather and I once heard a Montana rancher boast that out in his country they had "11 months of winter and a durned cool spring." As for myself, I creak at the joints during a cold snap and come in from doing the morning chores with icicles on my mustache. There are also a couple of toes that start aching to remind me of a far-off winter spent doing convoy duty on the North Atlantic. Despite these drawbacks, I'd hate to live in a climate where there wasn't *any* cold weather. There are sights and sounds and smells which are an inseparable part of the season. And there are certain jobs to be done on a country place which are just naturally cold weather jobs—and I enjoy doing them. Last week end, for example, George and I put in an afternoon felling trees and that's a chore I certainly wouldn't want to tackle during the month of August. Our neighbor on the far hill had told me he'd be glad to have us take out a row of elms and sycamores which had grown up along his fence line and were sapping the fertility from one of his fields, as well as blocking our view of the river. So we honed up our axes and took the cross-cut saw and hiked down across the creek and went to work. It wasn't a very cold day and George and I were soon down to our shirt sleeves, for there's nothing like a double-bitted axe to get the circulation going. We'd notch the tree on the side where we wanted it to fall, then bite into the other side of the trunk with the saw and soon the tree would come crashing down. Next we'd trim off the limbs and haul them down to a pile on the river bank.

*   *   *

The river, down where we were working, was frozen all the way across except for a few airholes. There was a thin covering of snow on the ice and we could see tracks where cottontails had ventured along the bank. A raccoon had been prospecting around the mouth of the creek and his tracks finally wandered off across the river, carefully skirting the airholes. There were quail tracks up in the field and Old Mac must have found the covey and flushed it, for late that evening I heard the Bob-whites whistling the covey-call as they got together again for the night. There's all kinds of feed and cover, so there's little danger for this covey even when they become separated. We have, however, seen a new pair of hawks hunting down our valley and up in the orchard above the house. I haven't had a chance to identify them but they have the ashy gray-blue color which is common to both the Duck Hawk and the Marsh Hawk—and both are real bird hunters. George reports having seen them catch songbirds up in the orchard.

*   *   *

If they are Duck Hawks, they are rather rare in Missouri. Or at least it's been a long time since I've identified a pair. These are the true Perigrine Falcon which gained fame in the Middle Ages when falconry and hawking was the sport of kings. In contrast to the Marsh Hawk, which kills some birds but is also of tremendous value as a rodent destroyer, the Duck Hawk's diet consists solely of birds. He is, however, so rare that his depredations could hardly become serious. We also have a pair of Cooper's Hawks and I'm laying for these rascals, for they are great killers of songbirds.

*   *   *

Well, I've gotten side-tracked from my wood-chopping, just as George and I did several times when we stopped to unravel the story of the tracks in the snow. It was getting on toward dusk as we climbed back up the hill toward home and a glass of hot Tom and Jerry beside the fireplace. As we neared the house, we could smell hickory smoke from the chimney. My mind slipped back to far-off country winters when wood was the only fuel that we burned. A furnace was an innovation in those days and the one at Grandpa Hall's house burned chunks of wood split just small enough so you could push them in through the furnace door. They'd haul that wood in from the farm in blocks sawed from the trunks of trees, and we'd split it after it got there. On very cold mornings when the sap was frozen, it was easy to split if you knew the knack of studying the grain and then giving the axe just the slightest twist as you brought it down on the end of the block. Most of the wood was oak and that was easy going until you got up to where the limbs started.

Recently when the thermometer dropped down close to the zero mark, the moon was in the last quarter and still bright as day when we got up in the morning. I'd pull on a wool shirt and step out on the terrace for a handful of fireplace kindling and hear the roosters crowing lustily down in the chicken house. And there would be the moon sailing clear and bright and heading down toward the western horizon, over beyond the river. Every branch of every tree and each blade of grass would be completely covered with frost which glistened in the moonlight. Far over across the valley, white frost on the big timber created the illusion of a scene from some old fairy tale or a setting for the "Ice Maiden" ballet. I'd forget the bitter cold and stand there for a while, watching the clouds in the eastern sky turn to pale rose color in the early dawn. Then I'd head back for the house and breakfast before the open fire and decide that maybe winter wasn't such a bad season, after all.

Signs of Spring

I'm certain from years of experience that there's bound to be more winter, but on this first day of March it is hard to believe. And this even though Mama and I have just come home to Possum Trot from Chicago where the snow was falling. But signs of spring are unmistakable and we know that once again the eternal cycle is starting. There is, for me, no season of the year when the earth is not alive; a voice to whom you can listen, even in her silences; an all-powerful being to whom you can speak in times of trouble, capable of bringing peace to troubled heart or mind; a friend in gentle mood to those who are her friends; and sometimes an enemy in storm or flood, when we have abused her for too long. "Staff of life and feeder of living things, innumerable are the hungry mouths that sap your vital essence"; that is the way one of my readers puts it, in a deeply understanding song to the land. Today is a day ill-suited for being shut away with pencil and sheaf of clean, white paper for setting down these random thoughts; or for writing those necessary letters about where to go fishing or when the warblers will start back north or why the possum likes peanut butter!

*   *   *

Outside the study in the pin oak tree, the nuthatch is sounding his little tin horn as he searches head-down for insects and small cocoons and borers under the bark. All day the cardinal has been singing. Over in the cedars on the hillside, the mockingbird is practicing his spring sonatas in a soft, reflective voice; doubtless he wants to be ready when his prospective bride arrives. The woodpeckers fly back and forth from one big tree to another with their stiff wing feathers whistling; calling back and forth in tones that are cheerful, even though raucous. The jays, who have many notes but only one that is musical, have dispensed with all the others in honor of such fine weather. All morning long whenever we'd hear a song that had been silent since last summer, we'd look for the Carolina wren. And sure enough, there he'd be, sitting atop one of the cross rails on the fence and trying out one of his innumerable small lyrics.

The birds are coming back, all right. On Saturday the first white-throated sparrow appeared at the feeder and since then has been back several times, although we haven't heard him sing. He is one of the beauties among all the sparrows and perhaps the sweetest singer of them all. He is easy to recognize from his white throat, three lateral white stripes on the head and a yellow spot between his eye and bill. The white-throat seldom if ever nests this far south, but he is here sometimes until June first before moving northward to his nesting grounds which reach as far as Hudson Bay. I note that March tenth is given as his normal arrival date in Missouri, but Guy Greenwell tells me that he'd seen several out north of Columbia even before ours had arrived. The fox sparrow is here, too, although only a spell of real winter weather will bring him in to the feeders. For the rest of the time, he stays down in the ravine where the undergrowth is heavy; and if you're careful you will find him scratching in the leaves and making them fly. Still another arrival and a rare one, although he was discovered by the Comforts who are better birdmen than I will ever be, is the Leconte's Sparrow which they have found twice in the heavy cover at the foot of our road. Last

Sunday, as we drove south into Illinois on one of the most interesting bird expeditions in all my experience, we saw many red-winged blackbirds and a pair of red-shouldered hawks. Both these birds are occasionally reported in Missouri as winter residents but these were my first of the season and I'll set them down as signs of spring!

*　　　*　　　*

On one of these warm days we're going into the beehives for a look. One of our hives particularly must have started into the winter with a young and prolific queen for that hive is always busy on warm days. I'd say, and my friend Mahoney can check me if I'm wrong, that some of those bees sailing about in the sunshine must be youngsters learning to fly. There are others who come down to drink from crevices in the rock walls which are always moist this time of year—and still others which seem to be bringing in pollen from some of the earliest shrubs. We want to check the "supers" on these hives to make sure there's plenty of honey to carry them through until the flow really starts. And on the other hand, if those supers are still full, we know that new supers filled with fresh beeswax "foundation" ready to be drawn into comb must be added to the hives extra early. If we don't do this and the hives get crowded, with little space for storage, there is almost sure to be trouble with swarming when May rolls around.

*　　　*　　　*

The daffodils think spring has already arrived, for they've pushed up a full six inches on the southwestern slopes. Field daisies and Queen Anne's-lace, those hardy perennials, are turning green with new leaves. Lilac buds are starting to swell and the tassels are appearing on the aromatic sumac, while tiny new leaves are showing on the climbing roses. Well— Mama and I will miss some of Missouri's spring this year. We're heading eastward next week for the North American Wildlife Conference in New York, where the subject will be "The Place of Wildlife in a Changing World". That is an interesting subject indeed, and a discussion in which I'm glad to be able to take part. But meanwhile the biddies are waiting to be fed and there's a stint of firewood to be chopped before supper. I'd better be at it.

Summer's Flowers Begin to Bloom

The recent rains here filled our pond with four feet of water, a good start toward its full nine-foot depth. They also shattered the fading blossoms of the spring wildflowers, except for a few hardy fellows like the wild phlox where it grows in the sunny fields. But some of the summer flowers, such as bergamot or "horse mint," are already blooming and the trees have the tropical lushness of early summer. Shrubs and vines are putting forth long shoots of growth. Rock plants make a solid green carpet over the garden walls, while all the annuals Mama has planted have taken hold without an hour's setback and are off to a wonderful start. The red honeysuckle along the fence is blooming its head off and the Paul's Scarlet climbers are a mass of color. Even the small bed of hybrid tea roses — red and pink and yellow — have bloomed this year ahead of all the pests which ordinarily make them such a care. Now the main problem is to keep them picked. Last night, the fireflies flickered in uncountable numbers. The chorus of "spring peepers" — a second crop, by the way, — came from the creek and from away over by the pond in the far field. We stayed outdoors for a long time listening to them and to the song of the toads. There were several of these latter singing — or rather, several varieties. One has a voice pitched in the middle range, with a short song of only a few notes.

*　　　*　　　*

Another sings a melody that is a long, high-pitched trill; it is truly musical but in a way impossible to describe. Perhaps it needs a country ear to interpret it as musical, although there are many who will agree that these songs are among nature's sweetest sounds. There was one which tuned up after we'd gone to bed that we hadn't heard before. It sang a distinct single note, pitched rather low and repeated three times at well-spaced intervals. But I was too sleepy by that time to go a'hunting to find what species of toad or frog had produced this new spring song. There are some who find the toads or frogs repugnant, but frogs are bug-eaters with marvelous appetites and the more of them we have, the better we like it.

Every day new birds arrive. This morning's traveler was the

yellow-breasted chat. If the bird world contains one individual with a sense of humor, it is certainly this biggest member of the warbler family with his totally un-warbler-like song. He picks the most conspicuous place he can find for his performance; and at Possum Trot this is the highest twig of a big sycamore tree down by the garden. If you have patience to slip up quietly and then stand still, he will soon come out in plain sight and go into his act. He cocks his head and droops his wings and waggles his tail, all the while sending forth a series of clucks, quacks, whir'r'rs and mews that are sure to set you laughing. Then, like as not, he will take off in a queer, dancing flight to some other tree near-by, singing as he goes. It hasn't been easy this season to identify the birds as they come in, except by their songs, for the foliage is too dense. Our Carolina wrens, which wintered here and pre-empted the swinging bluebird house for their first brood, have cast them out into the world, and are ready to go to work again.

*   *   *

Sometimes I wonder what's the excuse for writing about such seemingly inconsequential matters as Carolina wrens and tree toads in days when the world sometimes seems like a huge incendiary bomb with the time-fuse steadily ticking away. It isn't because of a desire to escape today's realities; indeed, I think that anyone whose mind does not dwell, now and again, upon the sorry state to which we human beings have brought our world is either a fool or a moron. We have sold ourselves a set of shoddy values based on folly and half-truths and by these we live. We mistake materialism for progress and if we have the knack for accumulating goods, which can even be found among packrats and jays, we take unto ourselves the credit for having brought the blessings of science to a waiting world.

*   *   *

We boast of the benefits which accrue to men in cities. We talk in city terms about the "sciences" of economics and sociology, never stopping to consider whether we have so violated the natural laws of man's relationship to his environment that sociology and economics, which are not sciences, can never cure man's ills.

Perhaps the contemplation of a pair of Carolina wrens or a cardinal singing in the top of a white oak tree, or of a wildflower growing in a sun-drenched field, is not enough to cure the madness which is leading surely toward man's self-imposed destruction. Perhaps, on the other hand, it may lead some of us back to an understanding of eternal verities —both natural and spiritual—in which alone lies our salvation.

 *Langston Hughes*

Winter Moon

How thin and sharp is the moon tonight!
How thin and sharp and ghostly white
Is the slim curved crook of the moon tonight!

Langston Hughes was born February 1, 1902, in Joplin, Missouri. Immediately after high school graduation he left for Mexico, returning to the United States to study briefly at Columbia University. He worked his way to Paris, where he stayed for a year before going on to Italy and Spain and back to New York and Washington, D.C. He worked there as a busboy while he wrote poetry, developing the distinctive style—touched by jazz and the blues—that was to set his work apart. His first book, "The Weary Blues," won the First Prize for Poetry offered by *Opportunity* magazine in 1925, and Lincoln University in Pennsylvania honored him with an honorary doctorate in 1943. He died in 1967, leaving his name secure among American poets.

Dream Variations

To fling my arms wide
In some place of the sun,
To whirl and to dance
Till the white day is done.
Then rest at cool evening
Beneath a tall tree
While night comes on gently,
     Dark like me—
That is my dream!

To fling my arms wide
In the face of the sun,
Dance! Whirl! Whirl!
Till the quick day is done.
Rest at pale evening . . .
A tall, slim tree . . .
Night coming tenderly
     Black like me.

Cross

My old man's a white old man
And my old mother's black.
If ever I cursed my white old man
I take my curses back.

If ever I cursed my black old mother
And wished she were in hell,
I'm sorry for that evil wish
And now I wish her well.

My old man died in a fine big house.
My ma died in a shack.
I wonder where I'm gonna die,
Being neither white nor black?

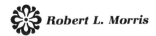 **Robert L. Morris**

The Bloody Brothers

Long time ago I knowd Maw Tabor, lived to herself up agin Cattle Hill. She never come to town but to buy tea an' coffee an' sugar an' sech like twict a year. She had no kin on this land, but that stalled her no whit frum a-talkin' with them she loved. Her ol' man crossed Jurdan fifty year agon I guess, but she set most ever night a-gossipin' to him afore the harth far. In summer she'd set on the back steps under the stars an' sky a-doin' the same thing. He went by a kick frum a mule as nateral-like as God's critters ever went. So she talked nateral to her ol' man.

But her two boys went off in a way agin nater so to say, an' she ain't never got over hit. So she talked to them like a crazed critter ur somelike a wise woman maybe.

Nights when the storm wus high an' wind wus fallin' like wrath, ur when lightnin' slit the sky ur thunder smote earth, then you could hear her a-talkin' to Jim an' Jake. That wus her boys' names. She would set afore the harth flames in her black cabin up thar on the hill two mile frum no whur an' she'd talk an' keep on at hit long as God kep' the stirrin' up thar in heaven.

Whut she said to them boys none never come to know, cause hit wus all in a witch woman's tongue, an' if 'twus fur good nur evil none could never know. But she said 'twus evil, seein' all the hard ways that come over us, I guess hit wus.

Onct Bill Furner got bold an' ask her whut she wus a-sayin'—come right out like that as brazen an' ask her—she give him a word that frize all blood in him. An' her ol' black cat

---

Robert L. Morris was born in Indiana in 1902 and, after earning a B.A. at the University of Arkansas, studied at the University of Iowa and Chicago, but he has spent most of his life in the Ozarks. A poet and the author of dialect tales, he was for many years a professor of English at the University of Arkansas, where he wrote and produced a number of plays for the University theater. He makes his home in Fayetteville.

jumped down frum the rafter an' bunched up hits back an' walked on hits toes. An' ol' Maw Tabor spit baccy in the far, an' hit leaped out with two arms an' wellnigh cetched Bill Furner atween 'em. So that wus the last time a body wus so foolish like that.

But we all knowed she had a back room in that thar house an' hit had the blood stains frum her two lads still on hit. None could see 'em, but they wus thar on the floor—two big pools, clotted blood it wus, as big as warsh tubs. They wus thar, cause Andy Lapp whut's gone to his rest many a year now seen 'em thar while Jim an' Jake laid white an' bleedin' in their mother's arms, jist atter they kilt Hank Carson frum behind the valley.

They'd been feud agin Hank an' his sence afore their gran'paw's time. So when Hank come pesterin' round they wus naught fur hit but let things head up. That mornin' Hank come prowlin' round, an' ol' Maw Tabor, she says to Jim an' Jake. "Thar he is agin," says she to her boys. "Hit's him an' his that kilt your gran'pap." An' she laid them their guns in their arms. An' when Hank Carson seen them a-takin' aim out the winder, he up an' shot Jake Tabor point blank, an' he fell in that room an' soaked in his blood.

But Jim, he had a steady nerve, an' he pulled an' shot that Hank Carson plum through the right eye. But when he done that, Hank's ol' Uncle Lem stepped frum behind the brush an' let pore Jim have two right 'tween the eyes. An' he rid off a-draggin Hank Carson's carcas. An' Jim Tabor wus a-layin' on the floor makin' another puddle big as a warsh tub.

Ol' Maw Tabor wus a-seein' this frum her doorstep, an' when Lem Carson got his back half-way hid in the trees up the hill, she pulled up her gun an' give him one right sharp 'tween the shoulders, an' he felled down frum his horse, an' rolled down the rocks, a-draggin' Hank's clay. An' down thar in the gully they laid too, an' the buzzards had many a rich feast, so Andy Lapp told me.

She wus a stout, strong woman, an' she drug them two lads frum that back room, an' laid 'em in the ashes afore the harth. Then she went to the back room whur them blood blots wus, an' she said, "Thar's my two boys. I keep 'em allus by me." Next day she had them two lads put down in the grave yard under the hill. Then she drug planks into the back room, an' with hammer an' some nails she built a floor an' laid hit crost the floor whur the blood wus. She kept the blood on that floor jist as hit flowed frum her sons' white bodies.

An' that's why you hear her a-talkin' in a dark tongue on storm nights when you dare up the hill to listen. She talks to them she calls her boys in the back room. But when a stranger comes, you'd never know she keeps two lads in that thar room. You'd never know she hold feud agin no man. Cause all is quiet, an' the floor to the back room is clear an' open as boiled pigs' feet.

But us round hyar knows they's two blood clots black an' big as warsh tubs on that floor, an' them she calls her lads.

 *Ward Allison Dorrance*

Notes for a Prayer

To Be Recalled at Thanksgiving

Lord:

I've thought this over. There is no reason to recast it in conventional terms. I'm a fresh hand. But I'm sensitive to style. And I don't like the tone adopted in prayer. That meekness. That muted buzz-saw monotony. Seems to me that just plain sincerity ought to breed more conviction. And spontaneity should have some weight. Children probably know exactly how to set about it. Children and old-time darkies.

If your complaint department is as short-handed as I suspect it is, You'll smile to get this. You'll want to mark the day with a white pebble. Or maybe You use stars for that. The tarnished ones that wouldn't be quite up to a June night. Because I'll wager that most of what you hear is in the manner of Letters to the Times. Old gentlemen who denounce things with a Latin quotation. Ladies with whale bone stays in their collars and in their prose style. Anyway I'll bet You rarely get thanked for anything except by way of preface to a new request. I don't want anything.

This is pure gratitude.

The lanes were sweet with honey locust last spring. And clouds lay high, banked from the level dewpoint. One day when the mourning doves were blowing in those hollow reeds of theirs, I spent a whole day on the bluffs over Rocheport. I

Ward Dorrance was born in Missouri, April 30, 1904. He graduated from the University of Missouri and returned from military service and travel abroad to teach there. He is the author of a novel, *The Sundowners. The White Hound*, published by the University of Missouri Press in 1959, brought together the stories of Dorrance plus a collection by Thomas Mabry. *A Man About the House*, a novella, was published in 1972. On its initial appearance, the title story had won Dorrance an O. Henry Short Story Award. He has made his home in Georgetown in the District of Columbia.

didn't do a darned thing but watch ducks. Fifty-three of them down on the river. They'd swim upstream a couple of feet, then, still facing upstream, drift back three. Then they'd start up again, and each duck's breast touched the apex of a little cone of wake. The water was striated so by each duck's paddling. Now and then one of them would lift himself out of the water far enough to flap his wings. Suddenly, out of the idling flock, one would swim like a flash to the bank. Probably saw a baby frog. I can't think of anything else that would make a duck put in such licks for the shore.

A lot of important people were doing a lot of big things while I was watching ducks. That's half the trouble. They go messing around stirring up things. By now they're used to it and think trouble's normal. Like people by the boiler factory who can't sleep at night for the quiet. Big people ought to be forced to watch ducks. It might help us all. And I don't see how it could do the ducks any harm.

Not that they could watch ducks as well as I did. Not right off. Not without practice. I took hours for each duck. It took time to mull over each one carefully. Yet all that time I wasn't actually concentrating on ducks.

I recalled that the Osages had named the river below me *Ni-sho-dse*, The Murky Water. I wasn't surprised to find myself remembering such things. The Osages and I are just like that; like two crossed fingers. . . . Then I fell to thinking of how Arrow Rock lay upstream a few bends around to my right. Whether you say it in English or *Pierre à la Flèche* in French, it's a right pretty name. From that point it was no trouble at all to imagine Kit Carson meeting Mr. Washington Irving on the brick sidewalk before the tavern there . . . to think of Dan Boone's sons floating off salt in logs . . . of Bingham painting his *Jolly Flatboatman.* And then there was Old Franklin close, too: and wagon trains pitching off in the ruts for Santa Fe.

. . . Downstream lay the fort of Côte-sans-Dessein. I smiled to think how Madame Roy used all the water and all the milk and how she still found something to put out the fire the Indians set. Her husband was mad as all get out when the smart alecks of Saint Louis offered her a silver pot in commemoration.

Sometimes it wasn't my head that thought, but my leg. Or my arm, as the sun beat down on it, as the wind flattened the small hairs of my wrist. That was as good a way to think as any. It didn't interfere with my gratitude.

I hope it doesn't escape You that what I am doing here is an act of faith, of thanks. A sort of vote of confidence. And is it plain that I am asking for nothing that I don't already have?

With due respect, I hope you will do nothing more for me but just go on away and leave me alone. I renounce the time you might have spent on me. It can be used on the Legislature. Or the D.A.R.'s. Singly they're fine folks. But collectively they pass resolutions.

The ducks and I don't want anything changed.

Be good enough to leave us as we are, in Missouri.

 *Don West*

Ribbon

A thin, brown mare was grazing the winter wheat with the fatter, younger stock.

"Whoa, Ribbon," said her owner, a young man, who was also a newcomer to the Ozarks.

When we walked up to her she raised her head, looked at us calmly, and then went back to grazing. Her brown coat did not shine in the November sun. Her mane was scanty and where the collar had rested in front of her withers there was a short tuft of sparse hair, which tried to fall on the wrong side of her neck. Despite her drab appearance, I thought she was pretty. And, proof of her fertility, her last year's mule colt was there for me to see. I was, nevertheless, disappointed. "But what can one expect to get for a heifer calf?" I asked myself.

"She's too slow to work with our other horses," said her young owner. "But she'll work. You have to keep after her."

I looked at Ribbon from all angles From the front I noticed the narrowness of her shoulders and the gentle look in her eyes.

"She has a nice face," I said, wondering if she were actually going to be mine.

From the side I was less pleased. Extra high withers accentuated the thinness of her long neck. Her ribs showed and between the muscles of her rump there were deep grooves.

The owner held her by the mane, while I opened her mouth to look at her teeth—a gesture on my part because I knew I could tell nothing about a horse's age by looking at its teeth. I saw that she did have teeth and let her go back to grazing.

Don West was born in Oklahoma on September 12, 1905. He attended Southeast State Teachers College in Durant, Oklahoma, and the University of Arkansas and taught school in Arkansas and Alaska. Before the move to the Ozarks, he was associated with the art movement in Santa Fe, New Mexico, in which his brother Hal was a central figure. *Broadside to The Sun*, published in 1945 and from which the following selection is taken, was illustrated by Hal West. West lives in Fayetteville, Arkansas.

"How old did you say she was?" I asked.

"I don't know. We bought her for nine, two years ago. I think the man lied. I think she's more like twelve or fifteen now."

"Can she eat corn?"

"Yes, but we always feed her soft food."

"No blemishes, no lameness anywhere?"

"She's sound as a dollar," he said, smiling. "Work anywhere you put her. And the sweetest horse that ever dirtied a britchin'."

I grabbed the mare's tail and gave it a hard yank to one side, as I had seen horse traders do. Ribbon did not show enough resistance, I thought.

"How's her bowels?" I asked. "I notice she's a little soiled behind."

"She has the runnin's-off sometimes."

I wished I did not have to have a horse; I also wished for more money to get one. I thought for a long time; I knew I would be parting with a fine heifer if I traded. But I was not getting anywhere wishing and pondering. Finally I said, "Let's take her in; I want to get on her and ride a little."

To hesitate for fear of making a mistake was worse, I thought, than making a mistake. That was why I had just bought the old Spence place in lonesome Horrigan Hollow. I could not lose much on that. Now all I could lose was a beautiful heifer calf, worth fifteen or twenty dollars.

"It's hardly possible," said the young man, as we went with Ribbon toward the barn, "but she could have a colt this season. It's been twelve months since she was bred."

"I won't count on it," I said. "I'll breed her in the spring."

At the barn he put a blind bridle on the mare and folded two gunny sacks for a blanket. He got an old saddle off a hook. The iron stirrups clanged against each other. The girth was made of gunny sacks; there was no leather on the horn; the skirt was hard and curled and broken. I was to borrow the saddle and bridle if I decided to trade so I could ride home, a journey of fifteen or sixteen miles.

I mounted the mare and kicked her into a trot for a turn around the premises. It was so delightful to be on a horse's back I decided to make the trade. And, after eating a little lunch and being given some cookies to put in my pocket, I rode away. The young man called after me, "You can just keep the saddle."

I could hardly believe in the sudden turn of events. Three hours before, when the young man and his mother had ridden up in their car to our little farm to look at the heifer, I did not have a horse, and knew of none I could trade for. Now I had a horse—was riding my own brown mare along a strange road fifteen miles from home.

The sun was not over two hours high. I should, I thought, be able to get home a little after dark. Then I would light the lantern to show my wife and two children the new horse.

I was having a good time. A man on a horse is, in spite of embarrassing rope reins and a gunny-sack blanket, still a horseman, and can look down and smile upon all pedestrians. However ragged the saddle he can still leap from it and leap into it, even if his mount does not make a quick get-away.

On first starting out, one slap with a stiff little oak switch on the mare's rump sent her trotting. This trot was more suitable for a buggy than a saddle but I enjoyed the jolts. The mare pointed her ears, picked up her feet, and set them down. I leaned on the pommel of the old saddle and felt the wind pass my cheeks. Then suddenly the jolting became more severe as Ribbon's steps shortened. She bounced back into a walk. This gave me a chance to rest my legs and I sat lazily in the saddle, watching the slowly shifting scenes in the brightly tinted woods. Leaves were falling through the sunlight and shadows. I could hear cowbells clanging, a woman calling "Soooook."

Then I noticed that Ribbon's head was so low she looked as though she were grazing. And her steps were almost as slow as those of a grazing horse. I kicked her, jerked the reins, and switched her again. She backed her ears and went into a trot. I hit again and she went faster. "We've got to get home, old girl," I told her. We passed through the sunny spots on the winding road at a thrilling speed. But we had not gone far at this rate when the jolting began—a warning that the trot was ending and the walk was coming. This time she had not trotted as far as she had the first time.

Now her walk was even slower, enough slower to make me realize it was going to be a fight to get home in time to show my wife and children the new horse before they went to bed. But I remembered the warning of the young man, "Don't ride her too hard; she's just grass fed."

My mare had a way of walking that was new to me. She

moved as though she said, "Now this step will certainly be the last; no, I'll take just one more."

I looked at the sun which was getting low and beginning to turn a little red. Clustered around it was a group of ugly dark clouds.

It required harder licks with the switch to get the same amount of trotting. Naturally the switches wore out faster and I had to stop more often to break them off. The sun went down, dusk came, cold and moist, and night fell rapidly because the clouds were by that time covering the sky. I was still a long way from home—eight or ten miles.

We were out of the woods going along lanes; bushes with switches were hard to find. Several times I rode up to a thorn bush thinking it might be an oak or an elm. I went on past houses but I did not stop. I did not want to tell my tale and ask for food and shelter. And when finally we reached the highway long after dark, all the things that had been progressing—the approach of the storm, the mare's exhaustion and complete callousness, and my worry—reached a peak. I sat on Ribbon as she stood still on the pavement; she would not go another step. A cold wind cut through my thin clothes and rain began to fall.

I supposed Ribbon had stopped there because she had seen the barn, for there was a big barn to my left which I could see only dimly. And near by on a knoll was a house. There were no lights. As it was still early in the evening I decided the people must be away. I got off the horse and tried to open the gate to the barn lot but I could not figure out how to open it. So I tied the mare to the fence, climbed over, and ran toward the barn. Just as I got inside the door the storm came with all its fury. I had never heard harder rain and wind. Whipping, howling, roaring, it went on deafeningly without letting up for what seemed like half an hour. During a lull I went down to try again to open the gate but came back completely baffled. I thought about the mare as I relished my own shelter. She was already tired and hungry, and now she was wet and cold as well.

It was so dark in the barn I could see nothing. Some creature was breathing enormously at my elbow. I hoped it was a cow rather than a bull. I sat on the pulverized manure and leaned against the slatted wall. I rolled a cigarette and smoked it. Finally I decided to crawl up in the loft and lie down in the hay. I could not find the ladder; so I crawled up the wall by putting my toes between the boards. Lying down, hungry and worried, I did not hope to go to sleep. Would someone steal my horse? What would the people think when they came home? Would they come looking for me? Would they be kind?

Cars roared by, their headlights brightening the interior of the barn. The rain stopped altogether. Then finally I heard an old car with a chugging motor stop at the gate where Ribbon was tied. I heard voices and I could easily imagine what they were saying. I was in an unreasonable hurry to make myself known before they started searching and, because it was difficult to climb down backward, I jumped, hitting slushy manure at the entrance of the barn. I fell and hurt my leg. I had to limp going up to the house and I was shuddering from cold and pain. Two dark figures were going toward the house.

I met the driver of the car in the garage. I had not talked long when the man started laughing. Everything about me was funny to him I guess; I had a black beard several weeks old, my teeth were chattering, and I had just jumped out of his barn loft.

"So you jumped!" he said, and laughed. All the way down to the gate he laughed and it made me feel very comfortable to hear him. I was being taken care of and laughed at. The stars were shining now but the wind was still blowing hard.

He untied Ribbon, led her to the gate, and opened it.

"I couldn't open the gate," I said.

"And you couldn't open the gate!" he said, laughing again. He had a good, heavy, hard kind of laugh, like his body and face. "Why, all you do is just push down on this pole and the gate raises clear o' the ground and then you swing it around. This is the only kind of a gate to have."

He led Ribbon under the big open shed where I had longed to put her.

"I'll git her some corn," he said. He produced an old washtub out of the darkness, opened a crib door, and got some ears of corn; and as he shucked it he threw it in the tub. Ribbon was nickering softly.

"How old is she?" he asked.

"Anything from eleven to fifteen. I don't know. She may be twenty."

"She doesn't look old."

We stood and looked at her a while, though about all we could see of her was the outline of her body and the glistening of the water on her. She looked almost fat and very slick, too, being so wet.

"What'll you take for her?"

"Why, I've just traded for her. Gave a fine heifer calf for her. I've got to have a horse. And it's not often you can find one so cheap."

"I've got to have a horse, too," said the big man. He wasn't laughing any more. "I'd sure nuff buy her from you, if you'd price her right. Would you take twenty-five dollars for her?"

"Later, maybe, but it would not seem right at all not even getting her home. My wife and kids want to see her."

"Haven't been in this country long, have you?" he asked me as we went up toward the house.

"Two years. I'm from New Mexico."

"I'm from Oklahoma."

"I thought you sounded like an Oklahoman. I was raised there."

We stepped up on the front porch. "We'll see the old man," he said, in a low voice, letting me know for the first time that he was not the master of the house. Then he opened the door and showed me into a room, a stuffy old-fashioned room, with a double bed, a cluttered dresser, and old enlarged photographs on the walls. The fireplace was sealed up, like most fireplaces in the hills, and a tall heating stove sat in front of it. An old man was sitting in a rocking chair and a middle-aged woman was standing against the wall. The old man did not smile at me but told me to sit down. He was enormous and shapeless with great breadth of shoulders and a big, heavy head that drooped. His nose was swollen and almost touched his upper lip. He had small, dull eyes that regarded me strangely with a mixture of amusement and suspicion.

"What did you say your name was?" he asked in a rumbling, quavering voice.

I told him and he puzzled over it a while, trying to make it mean something.

"Where do you live?"

"Two miles east of Winslow on Sunset Road."

"What place?"

"We bought it from Millard Pierce."

"Pierce . . . ?"

"From down on Big Frog."

"Must be George Pierce's boy."

"Maybe," I said.

"Who'd he git it from?" He asked this question of the carpet.

"Bob Patterson."

"Patterson . . . ?"

"Newcomers. He was a pretty big farmer in western Oklahoma. He bought an eighty up by the cemetery—state land."

"I cain't figure out what place you got," said the old man.

"It's part of the old Anderson tract. Nine acres."

"I know it!" he said, his eyes showing a little more light. "What'd you have to give for it?"

"Six hundred and fifty."

"What'd Pierce give for it?"

"Two hundred and fifty."

The old man made a noise in his throat and looked at the carpet. He was silent for a while and so were the two others, standing by the wall. Cold and nervous, I could not keep from shaking. Outside the wind howled.

"Married?" asked the old man as he brought his head slowly up and turned his face in my direction. There was a peculiar look in his eyes.

"Yes, I'm married, and have two children—a girl five, and a boy four."

The two younger people continued to watch us. The sympathy they showed in their wide eyes, the stiff way they stood, hinted that I still could be thrown out into the night. Even when the old man smiled at me very faintly, I saw that the young man and woman were yet uneasy for me.

"What did you do before you come to this country?"

"I was with the Museum of New Mexico. I restored pottery and drew pottery designs."

"Museum . . . pottery . . ."

After this there was a longer silence than ever.

"Well," said the old man at last, rather crossly, "what do you want to do?"

"What do you mean?" I smiled.

"Well, do you want to stay here all night or go on?"

I told him haltingly that I would like to stay. I informed him I had only a quarter in my pocket.

"I guess you can stay."

And then the woman spoke up. "Have you had any supper?"

I looked up; she had relaxed and was smiling. The young man, too, was no longer tense. I told them I had not eaten.

"Feed his horse, Cliff," said the old man.

"I've already fed it," said Cliff shortly and went out of the room with the woman.

I was left with the old man. He talked. There was a difference in his tone now.

"We've been to church. I cain't git around much any more and I don't never git off the place except to go to church once in a while. Somebody has to help me walk except for just toddlin' around in the house. I'm eighty-nine years old."

Fascinated by his great, awkward bulk, I watched him holding the arms of the rocking chair as though he might be riding a ferris wheel. Gradually I was gaining his confidence. He looked at me longer each time he turned his head. He had begun an account of his early life there in that house when the woman came and said, "It's ready."

The two younger people sat with me while I ate cold potatoes, bacon, corn bread, and drank skimmed milk. I learned that they had been married only a year and that she was the old man's daughter. There was much laughter from Cliff as he told his wife about my jumping out of the barn loft. I laughed too, though I still felt oppressed by the old man and the gloomy house. It seemed strange to see the woman's angular face lifted with restrained laughter.

"The old man came in an ace o'lettin' you out," said Cliff in a low voice. "He hates young men. He hates me but he'll talk to me. He likes to talk to anybody that'll listen."

"Why does he hate young men?" I asked.

"Because they can do things he cain't."

We might have talked longer after I ate but the dining room was cold. The woman fixed my bed in the room with the old man, who had got into bed while I was eating. She brought old quilts and rugs and threw them over the couch, a curved backless couch sitting on four lion's legs, the paws of which clutched glass balls. When I was under the weight of the quilts and the rugs and the room was dark, the old man's voice rumbled to me.

"I wish they had let me die last year. It'd be better 'n goin' on like this! They worked awful hard to save me. And I'd rather be dead. I cain't do nothin'. I'm as helpless as a baby. Go from chair to bed, and from bed to chair. . . ."

He did not say much more than that but he struggled to make his big body comfortable by tossing about and with each move there was a groan. When he was still, he had trouble breathing. I listened to his gaspings and blowings and tried to keep them from disturbing me. I could not help him and, though I wished he could be made young again, I thought as he did that such a life was not much fun. I wondered if he might die during the night. And when his heavy breathing could not be heard I became frightened. I listened, lifting my head from the pillow, holding my breath. Then I heard him breathing easily, slowly. I wondered how it felt to be so near death, waiting for the end like a condemned man and going from chair to bed, from bed to chair. . . .

Just before I went to sleep my mind went back to my mare as I remembered how shiny her wet coat looked in the starlight after the rain. I thought of my children. They would be happy to have a horse. I hoped we could soon move down into Horrigan Hollow. There was no other place to think of being any more. The nine acres where we were living no longer seemed like home. The mind takes hold of the unknown and will not let it go till it becomes the known.

*   *   *

I watched daylight come the next morning, and listened for sounds of life and activity. Soon I could tell that the old man was awake and I said "Good morning."

"Good . . . mornin'."

"How do you feel?"

"All . . . right . . . I guess."

"It's cold," I said.

"Damn cold! Why don't you . . . git up and build a fire?"

I crawled from under my pile of rugs and quilts and into my clothes. Everything I touched was icy cold. I found some newspaper and kindling.

"Twist it! Twist it!" said the old man crossly when he saw me crumpling the paper. Everyone has a different way, I thought, as I twisted the paper. There was not much kindling and it was too large. I had little hope of the fire burning and watched it anxiously. For a long time the fire crackled and fluttered and at last it got under way. When it did, the old man crawled out of bed, leaked in a gray pot close by, got jerkily into his pants and with short, tottering steps, like a baby learning to walk, covered the distance between bed and rocking chair. He fell heavily into its maternal lap, gripped its arms, and leaned forward toward the stove. All this was accomplished with a kind of casual recklessness. He eyed me with a not unfriendly gaze, as though my sleeping in the room with him had brought us closer together.

I could hear Cliff and his wife talking in their bedroom and after a while the kitchen stove rattled, as someone built a fire.

"I've lived my life right here on this place," said the old man. "And there's been some changes since I was a lad." He told me then about the bad roads, about the village of Fayetteville, about the Indians, about the wild deer, the turkeys. But all this was just making talk; he warmed to his subject when he got on his married life.

"I've had three wives in the last two years," he said and chuckled for the first time since I had been his guest. "I've had six altogether. My first wife died twenty-five years ago. That's her picture there behind you on the wall."

The enlarged photograph showed a young and handsome woman in a high-necked dress.

"She was beautiful," I said.

He made no comment and showed no emotion.

"I'd marry me another'n if I got the chance."

"What happened to the recent wives?" I asked.

"I got rid of 'em. Well, one run off. They wasn't no good. One tried to poison me. She put poison in fried rabbit. I wouldn't eat none of it. But it kept comin' to the table, and finally she said, 'I thought you like fried rabbit,' and I said, 'I do but not *that* fried rabbit!' Somethin' told me there was poison in it; but it kept comin' to the table and finally I ate one of the front legs. I don't know what made me do it. I ate it and it hit me all of a sudden. I got awful sick and turned right blind. I told her to go git help, and when the help come, I told that bitch to git out, and she got out.

"They all wanted to kill me. One slept with a knife under her pillow. She said she had it to protect herself. I said, 'What'd you marry me for?'"

"Why do you marry such women?" I asked.

"I cain't help it," he said. He was silent for a while and then went on. "One was a young girl just about seventeen years old. I thought she'd be just the one for me. I found her pickin' beans barefooted. I married her and slept with her one night and the next mornin' she run off with my car.

"You'd think," he said after another pause, "that I'd not want another one but I would marry again, I guess. I ought to be able to git me a good old woman, just a good old woman—not too old, just a good, hard-workin' woman."

When we went in to breakfast the old man was quiet and withdrawn. He sat around the corner of the table from me and I frequently felt his eyes on me. Did he hate me, too, because I was young? Cliff sat across the table. When he talked his voice was loud and all the time his blue eyes were wide and sort of frightened.

For breakfast we had hot biscuits, bacon, eggs, gravy, butter, honey, and strong coffee.While I ate I found it easy to talk. I told them about my plans to leave the little farm as soon as I could get a suitable tenant for the place.

"I'm tired of farming with a hoe and carrying wood on my back down the hill because the farm won't support a horse. I'm going down in the hollow where the range is good. I have eighty acres with about fifteen acres tillable."

"What place is it?" the old man asked.

"The old Spence place down in Horrigan Hollow. West of Winslow about two miles."

"Uncle Billy Spence! I knew him! He's been dead a long time. He got rich down there, they say."

"We bought the place from an old bachelor who tried it out and after a few months of loneliness made three propositions. He would deed it to anyone who'd give him a home, any woman who'd marry him, or he'd sell for one hundred dollars. My wife and I got excited about it; we heard it was worth five hundred. So we went down there. It looked pretty scary but we bought it. The bachelor went straight to the poor farm. He was a sick man, really. The only thing wrong with the place is the road."

After breakfast I followed the old man back to his room to tell him good-by. I offered him the twenty-five cents and he took it. But he said I did not need to send any more. He asked me to stop in to see him. I told him I would like to and left him holding to the arms of his rocking chair.

Cliff had already fed Ribbon. He went with me to the barn

where the mare was standing with lowered head. Her nose was running and she breathed noisily.

"She don't look so young and slick this morning," said Cliff.

"No," I said sadly.

I saddled Ribbon and we talked about the old man. Cliff enjoyed telling of the old man's failures. He had heard the story second hand from the women who had, beyond a doubt, married him for the farm. Sleeping with the old man had been worse than they expected.

"People think I married his daughter for the farm, too, but I didn't. I married her because she's a good woman!"

He told me about a fight he had had with her former husband.

"I knocked him clean off the six o'clock bus!" he said and burst into a loud laugh.

Riding away, I looked at the old house on the knoll and the meadow land below, a smooth, shallow bowl of land, some forty acres in size—a wonderfully large meadow for northwest Arkansas. It glistened with ice and sunlight. I would have enjoyed owning it. There were no smooth wide meadows where I was going.

On the way home through the bright, bitter cold I worried about the mare's breathing; her nose was running and she made a rattling, wheezing sound. In spite of this, after her night's rest, she trotted without much urging from me. Having a horse, any kind of a horse, gave me such a feeling of power that I looked into the future with confidence.

The highway made long curve after long curve before I saw landmarks that told me I was close to home. At last I turned off the pavement onto Sunset Road and went east up Westfork Creek.

A little before noon I turned down my own hill, rode across the log bridge over the creek, and then over the four-acre bottom field to the barn at the foot of the hill.

From the cabin on the hillside my wife and children saw me and the three of them came down the icy stone steps to the gate below. They came slowly, cautiously, Muriel holding the hands of Tim and Petra. They were glad to see me but it was the mare who drew their attention.

I had brought home cows and pigs and goats before; this was the first time I had brought a horse.

"She's pretty, Don!" said my wife. "What's her name?"

"Ribbon."

"Well, Ribbon, I hope you like it here." She patted the mare's lean jaws. Then turning to me, "But where did you spend the night?"

"It's a long story," I said.

We watched the children, chunky, brown-eyed Tim, and blond, curly-haired Petra. Tim gazed in wonder and kept his distance. Petra got closer and closer to the brown mare. Finally my daughter shyly walked up to the mare's head and with one white slender hand lightly touched her neck. Then Tim went up to Ribbon and stroked her, too. But it was Petra who stayed with me while I unsaddled the mare and put her in the log barn and fed her wheat shorts and a block of hay. We stayed in the barn and watched her for a long time.

 *Francis Irby Gwaltney*

Windy Spears

Windy Spears was a native of Charleston and, except for his service in France during what we then called the World's War and on another occasion a solitary trip to Little Rock, he had never been more than fifty miles from home. He came by his nickname honestly enough.

Windy lived on a pension, and because pensioned veterans were better off during the Depression than at any time in our history, he lived well. His house was painted every third year, and because that gleaming whiteness contrasted so sharply with the shabby gray of houses that hadn't been painted since 1929, it looked like a mansion. It was filled with children: Miz Spears, a compactly built little woman who had been a Sipes as a maiden, established herself as a champion during the early and middle twenties—she had a baby every eleven months. Most of them were big, heavy boys. Since each baby added something to the size of Windy's pension, and since Doc Bollinger delivered babies for a fee of ten dollars, and because Windy's wife and children raised most of the family's

---

Francis Irby Gwaltney was born in Saline County, Arkansas, September 9, 1921. He wrote:

"Son of Francis Boulanger Gwaltney, M.D., and Mary Effie Irby Gwaltney. Grandson of Francis Marion Gwaltney, Private, First Arkansas Mounted Rifles, CSA. Great-grandson of Francis Cravens, Colonel, First Arkansas Mounted Rifles. The entire Gwaltney family, both here and in Virginia, is fetished about the name 'Francis'; there have been some seventeen all told.

"I grew up at Charleston, Franklin County, Arkansas, where there was Miss Doll Means, the greatest English teacher who ever lived.

"I was a sergeant, Cavalry, during World War II. Then the University of Arkansas where I took a lone course in 'creative writing.' Then all those years of teaching. I'm an associate professor of English at Arkansas Tech University and here I shall remain."

Gwaltney published eight novels (the most recent of which are *Destiny's Chickens*, 1973, and *Idols and Axle Grease*, 1974), teleplays for *The Alfred Hitchcock Show*, *The Fugitive*, and *Dr. Kildare*, and several screenplays. He died in February 1981.

food in that three-acre vegetable garden behind the house, Windy didn't find children an expensive luxury.

Windy was a man of habit. He arose at 5:30, ate a ham steak and four basted eggs with grits and five cups of coffee, then went to town, a block away. He carried a cane as a part of his disability, although he had been gassed and there was nothing wrong with his legs. At the corner of Main Street—hereafter cited as the Street—and North Greenwood Street, he picked up a bottle cap from a supply washed into the storm drain by the rains, then he used his cane as a club. He could knock that bottle cap sailing. It always landed between the regular and ethyl pumps of Melmer Dunmore's Filling Station. Then he called on Melmer.

Windy didn't stay long. He, like everybody else in Charleston, didn't like Melmer. It's just that Melmer's establishment was en route to better things, and besides, Melmer willingly listened to Windy's lies.

At the Tourist Cafe, Windy had a cup of coffee. That required almost an hour, because Dock Frye, proprietor, was still serving breakfast to Onion Creek rowdies in town after having sold their produce; thus the conversation was often interrupted. Windy was fond of Dock because he obviously believed any lie anybody wanted to tell him.

The hotel, really a room-and-board, was Windy's destination. There he could spend almost any number of comfortable hours with the proprietor, Old Cat Murphy. They had been sweethearts when they were young, and early in the Depression, when Old Cat was still a widder woman, sometimes they would even flirt—wanly, of course.

Old Cat had become mildly sophisticated from having been in contact with those occasional travelers who alighted at the hotel overnight; thus she had a developed talent for making Windy feel as if he might not be entirely appreciated in Charleston. Old Cat was also the only person in Charleston who could call Windy a liar without hurting his feelings.

"You're a liar and the truth ain't in you, Windy Spears." Old Cat's grin was kind of soft and regular. "You'd lie on credit if you knew you could git cash for the truth."

Windy shrugged; he really didn't care. " 'Spect so."

"Even Miss Doll don't believe you, and she'll believe anybody."

Windy settled comfortably; he knew Miss Doll loved him.

Francis Irby Gwaltney / 88

"Well—I tell you, Cat, a man's gotta do something he gits a kick out of and ain't nothing sets me afire like a well-told lie."

Windy went home for lunch, and, surrounded by his battalion of children and his sturdy, uncomplaining wife, he related his adventures of the morning. That wife was one of those women who used her husband as both a symbol and a weapon, so to his children Windy was a tyrant to whom young people listened with rigid respect. It was easier that way; when on those four occasions he was obliged to use his razor strop on one of those monumental sons, the experience put him to bed for a solid week. Even the third son, he who became one of the first All-Americans produced by the University of Arkansas Razorbacks, didn't talk back to his father.

There was a nap after lunch, and then, at 1:30, Windy continued with his routine. That meant an hour of gospel singing at the cobbler's shop, Spreading Adder Benefield, Prop. It was a quartet, with Spread singing bass, J. O. Cone at baritone, Barney Stittchen at tenor, and Windy at top tenor. To judges of gospel singing, Windy was considered to be one of the best top tenors in Franklin County, north or south of the river. Indeed, the quartet had once sung a few nervous hymns on KFPW Fort Smith, and Windy was invited, via letter and even telephone, to join several groups and quartets who had commercial aspirations.

Thus Windy's life was serene. It was easy talk, satisfying song, and a firm domestic tradition. None of us were complaining listeners. We all knew he had never seen combat during the World's War; he was in a quartermaster outfit several miles behind the trenches and a canister of phosgene exploded. Windy somehow took a whiff or so before he recognized his error. We all knew that. So did Windy. But we never said so. The tales Windy told were such monumental lies that they were first class entertainment in an era when the Gem Theater was open only two nights a week.

I was never taught that Windy told the truth. My mother was crazy. She ambled about our tiny house and our small yard, and people pitied her and swore I was going to hell for raising myself with no father and a crazy mother. I was never taught that Windy was a liar. I didn't need to be.

I had good instincts.

So it wasn't I, nor was it any one of us who called Windy's hand. It was a stranger, that most contemptible of people during the Depression, a Yankee with a hard voice and eyes lighter than the color of his face. He was an engineer employed by the WPA to build a viaduct over the railroad at Doctor's Ford Creek. That engineer stayed at the hotel, and when he wasn't trying to make time with Miss Hettie McIntosh, he was trying the same thing with Old Cat Murphy. Perhaps it was pure malice or perhaps it was simply jealousy when Old Cat stopped her bottom-wiggling and her lisping and her lip-licking in the presence of Windy—it made no difference because the engineer wanted Old Cat and he hated Windy.

While the engineer simmered and Old Cat listened, Windy made his daily call. Old Cat never accused him of lying in the presence of either friends or strangers, and because Windy knew he was safe, he put on a better show at the hotel than he did at, say, the filling station or the cobbler's shop.

Events conspired against Windy but they didn't defeat him. The subject of this morning's talk just happened to match an event that has yet to be forgotten in the gentle flow of Charleston's history. "They chased that old boy all over France," Windy was saying. "Finally they holed him up in one of them old French castles. Châteauseases, the French called 'em. Well, Lord knows, the MPs carried billy clubs; they didn't know how to use a rifle. So they come to my colonel and said they needed a man with rifle experience, one that could drive a five-penny nail from fifty feet, one that's owned a rifle all his life. Well, my colonel—old Colonel Winfield from out here at Vesta; he died last winter and I was head guard at his funeral. Well, Colonel picked me and some old boy from Tulsa, Oklahoma, but that Tulsa boy couldn't make it; in fact, he died with the flu. So that left it up to me."

The WPA engineer didn't believe a word of it, and he had his mouth cocked to say so, but Windy kept a fast pace; thus the engineer didn't get his chance.

"I'll tell you right now, I was scared, but that feller in the château had done a lot of killing, women and children mostly, and everybody was getting excited, so I didn't have no choice. I had to get 'im. It taken a while, almost all day, but I done it. I didn't want to kill a feller American, so I had to get in a position where I could shoot his gun outta his hand. So I—"

The telephone rang, and in Charleston in 1938 a ringing telephone meant something. The phone was an upright attached to one of those accordion extensions, which meant that it could telescope as much as six feet into a room. Old Cat nodded to the engineer, who relinquished his contempt for Windy long enough to shove the phone at Old Cat. As a part of her sophistication she had developed her own distinctive way of answering the phone, "Mmm, neh-low. . . ." And she listened.

Windy continued with his story, because even if the engineer wasn't paying close attention now, he was in the room and Windy had an audience.

Old Cat shoved the phone back to the engineer. "Just a minute, Windy." In another town and in another state, that would have meant this: Shut up and listen. But in Charleston we were rarely rude to one another.

Windy hushed; he wasn't angry, nor were his feelings hurt. He knew Old Cat had heard something awful on that telephone or she would never have asked him to stop talking.

Old Cat went to the window and looked down the Street. "They'uz two men holding up the bank right now. That'uz Dock Frye looking for Pete McCarthy," our sheriff.

The engineer recoiled and muttered something ugly, but Windy, still enraptured perhaps by the delicious violence inherent in the tale he had been telling, said, "Now just take it easy." His voice had the artificial clarity of the sleepwalker's.

The engineer didn't hesitate. He stepped behind the desk and picked up a shotgun Old Cat kept there. He threw it to Windy, who had completely recovered his native cowardice by now and thus dropped the shotgun. Dazed, he picked it up. The engineer shoved a box of shells across the desk, and then he fetched up a .45 automatic Old Cat kept under the cash box.

"All right, loudmouth," the engineer said, "now's the time for you to either put up or shut up. I got a real fast Lincoln car and there's plenty of room on the fender for you to lay and use that shotgun."

Windy's voice was thin and horribly reedy: "I get a pension." And because he had produced what was generally considered a good excuse for inaction, he took a small breath of relief.

"Yeah, for being the biggest liar in the World's War." The engineer shoved Windy toward the door. "Now you going with me or do I find a real man?"

Windy later confessed to Old Cat and, indeed, to me that he didn't really remember leaving the hotel, and sure enough, when he installed himself, rather tentatively, on the fender of the Lincoln, he was gray with a fear that must have been near death, but somehow he poked the barrel of the shotgun between the fender and the right headlight.

That was when the robbers emerged from the bank. They fired several shots up and down the Street, and then they jumped into their Model A, a blue one with a rumble seat and a cloth top, and then they hurried on out of town. Windy flinched when the engineer fired up the Lincoln, and if he hadn't been quick to grab the headlight, Windy would have fallen off.

It might not have been a shooting match at all if the bank robbers hadn't turned left at Schoolhouse Hill. No children were injured; indeed, we paid no attention to the robbers at all, because the first bell had already rung and we were busy at play, getting in four more minutes before the second bell rang for books. One of the games the boys were playing was Pile, and to Windy it appeared as if several boys were grouped anxiously about somebody who had fallen before the robbers' guns. That was when Windy got hold of himself.

The robbers were overtaken when they crossed the tracks near the old Spessard place. It was a rough crossing and the driver lost control on the dirt road for perhaps twenty-five yards. He used his brakes, and the engineer rammed his Lincoln almost against the Model A's bumper. That was when, no more than twenty feet from his target, Windy fired his first shot.

The robbers fired back; Windy didn't have an easy time of it. He was unwounded, but the engineer caught a buckshot slug in his left thigh. The Lincoln's radiator was wrecked and steaming. Windy told me and Old Cat that he began figuring, right then, that he'd better shoot fast and straight or that Model A was going to leave the Lincoln behind. His next two shots did the trick.

Nobody was killed, and that made our history a little easier to bear. The robbers were taken to Doc Bollinger's hospital, and something like a hundred pellets of number six duckload were removed from their necks and scalps. The *Fort Smith Times Record* and *The Southwest American* sent a photographer down, and, watched by our entire population, Windy was pictured returning the money to Clyde Hiatt at the bank.

Another picture showed him, still holding the shotgun, in the company of his compact little wife and all those children.

That event changed the pattern of Windy's life. He never embellished upon the tale, and he was always quick to admit that he had been frightened out of his wits. Later, when he was no longer a hero but was instead that consumptive-looking little man with bright eyes who talked a lot, he refused to talk about the robbery at all.

"Why don't you ever want to talk about it anymore, Windy?"

He looked at me as if I were a fool. "You ever been shot at, boy?"

"No sir."

"Well, it ain't no fun." Windy mused a moment. "A man ain't fixing to get shot at for telling a little lie or two."

"No sir." I waited because I knew he had something else to say.

"If you or anybody else wants to know the truth about it, it'uz in the newspapers and it's been framed and hung in the courthouse. That's all anybody ever needs to know about it."

And as he grew older, another war produced younger men who came home to lie about their own military careers. Windy became something of a listener, and even when he was absolutely certain that these new liars were not made of that substantial old-fashioned cloth of his generation, he encouraged them, nodded at the right times, asked the right questions; he was, to the really good liars of the new generation, a father figure. It was a role he relished almost as much as the one he had played when he had pioneered twentieth-century lying in Charleston.

When he died, finally a victim of that phosgene accident, he left various mementoes of his life to his friends in Charleston. Colonel Pettibone received the campaign hat. The shoes went to Scrooge Wilkins. Spread Benefield, for one reason or another, got the gas mask. The mess kit went to Will Bumpers. I'll never know why he decided to leave me the rifle.

Windy was given a soldier's funeral. It was the biggest funeral Charleston had ever seen. The American Legion was out en masse, officious, their silly uniforms somehow appropriate, their perfect attendance medals ajingle. Even the governor attended. But the perfect touch was a complete surprise; somebody lost in that maze called the Veterans Administration must have known Windy, because when his tombstone was produced, it failed to list the military organization to which Windy had belonged. The Quartermaster Corps, some sentimental bureaucrat reasoned, couldn't have produced a man like Jasper Sue "Windy" Spears, so after his name came the simple words "United States Infantry."

With Spreading Adder Benefield in charge, a gospel quartet sang several hymns over Windy's grave. Windy had had no favorite hymn, but Spread did; thus the featured hymn was "Shout the Glad Tidings." We all agreed that the tune seemed right enough.

 **Edsel Ford**

About Grampa, Who Died Poor

My grandfather in his once-Spencerian hand
Cribbed by the cold which scotched his ancient bones
Wrote two-cent postcards out of Dixieland
To twenty kin and near-kin, Smith and Jones
And several mixed up of a foreign name,
Saying *Now I am free, I might arrange a trip* . . .
Ready to travel before the postman came:
Clothes in a parcel, medicines in a grip.
But those who answered said they had the flu,
Or were about to move, or *Maybe later;*
And he, having nothing, nothing whatever to do,
Got too old even for the elevator,
Much less the train—lamenting most, no doubt,
The forty cents it took to feel them out.

Edsel Ford was born in Eva, Alabama, December 30, 1928. When he was eleven, his family moved to Arkansas and settled near Rogers, where he attended school and spent the rest of his life except for time away at the University of Arkansas, the army, and a brief writing job in New Mexico. His books include *This Was My War* (1955), poems about his army days, especially those in Germany, and *Looking for Shiloh* (1968), winner of the Devins Award at the University of Missouri Press. Ford died on February 19, 1970.

 *Roy Reed*

An Ozark Gardener, 86, Awaits

Coming of the Greening Season

Hogeye, Ark., April 12, 1976—Spring is late in the Ozark Mountains this year. The oaks and the maples are only now risking a few pale green shoots, tentative little leaves that will not constitute much of a loss if another frost steals in some night on a villainous northwest breeze.

Ira Solenberger is also late this year. Practically everybody else at Hogeye has braved the hazard of frost and planted corn, onions, English peas, and Irish potatoes. A few, emulating the bold dogwood and redbud trees, which for more than a week have been blooming bright white and purple against the dark hills, have gone so far as to put out beans, squash, and even tender tomato plants.

But Mr. Solenberger, who is regarded as the best gardener in Washington County, has not plowed a furrow or planted a seed this year. Like the craggy old maple tree in front of his house, he finds that his sap is slow to rise this spring. It would not occur to him to blame it on his 86 years.

He Blames the Flu

"It's that old flu," he said yesterday. "Got it back in the winter and can't get rid of it. First time I've had it since 19 and 18."

Roy Reed was born February 14, 1930, in Hot Springs, Arkansas. He graduated from the University of Missouri School of Journalism and was a 1963-1964 Nieman Fellow at Harvard. He worked for a time for the *Joplin Globe* and the *Arkansas Gazette*, and then for fourteen years was a correspondent for *The New York Times*, working out of Atlanta, Washington, New Orleans, and London. Before moving to London, he specialized in coverage of the American South. His articles have appeared in *The New York Times Magazine*, the *Atlantic*, *US*, and many other national and regional publications. He lives now in Hogeye, Arkansas, with his wife Norma. Their two children are grown and gone. He teaches journalism at the University of Arkansas.

He opened the door of his heating stove and threw another chunk of wood on the fire. He closed it a little sharply and glanced out the window toward his empty garden.

The main thing going on in the rural South this month is vegetable gardening—either the contemplation of it, as Ira Solenberger is doing, or the actual plowing, fertilizing, and planting, as thousands of others, from Hogeye to the Tidewater, are doing.

A farmer might take an hour to talk presidential politics or to help a cow give birth, but the really urgent business for him, his wife, and all of the children who are old enough to keep their feet off the onion sets is getting seeds and plants in the ground to take advantage of the warming days. With a little luck, the sweet corn planted this week will have roasting ears ("roashnears," they are called here) on the table by the middle of June.

*   *   *

It is a pursuit that seeks every year to join and outwit that awful force that pushes the shoots from the oak's branches and that is even now turning Seth Timmons's meadow from brown to green and impelling swallows to build nests in weathered old barns.

The same force pushes Ira Solenberger out the door in a hat and coat, hunched against the biting bright air blowing up from the Illinois River, to kick the dirt and study the sky, and then retreat back to the house to throw another chunk of wood on the fire.

There is a poet up the road at Fayetteville who leaves his tobacco-ridden study and drives into the hills to absorb the coming of spring. He watches for Robert Frost's signs, the gold that is nature's first green, "her hardest hue to hold," and for private signs of his own that stir his senses and his spirit.

Ira Solenberger's mind runs less to poetry than to science and to the satisfying of a huge curiosity. He is an amateur magician, and he performs magic with plants as well as cards.

"Summer before last, I grafted some tomatoes on some poke stalks." Why? "Just to see if they would grow."

*   *   *

But when he talks of nature and growth, he uses words that Frost might have used, or Thoreau.

"Plow deep" he says. "There's one acre right under another acre. I plow both of them."

Nature wants to reproduce its kind. That's the only reason anything bears, to reproduce its kind. "Phosphorous makes things grow roots. If you get roots, you're going to get something else.

"I farm with a tractor. But when it gets rowed up and a-growing, I use a roan horse."

Mr. Solenberger dispensed his advice on gardening as he stood awhile in yesterday's morning sun. He pointed to the three and a half acres he cultivated last year. It produced strawberries, rhubarb, corn, tomatoes, squash, sweet potatoes, Irish potatoes, okra, green beans, watermelons, cantaloupes, radishes, onions, and cucumbers. He ate what he wanted, froze some, and sold the rest at a farmers' market in Fayetteville.

*　　　*　　　*

He pointed to a fallow patch and said, "That's where I had my watermelons last year." He spoke in a loud, professorial voice, as if addressing the cows at the top of the hill 150 yards away.

"They told me I raised the biggest watermelons in northwest Arkansas," he continued. "One of them weighed 83 pounds."

"I've had people ask me, 'What's your secret for raising watermelons?' I tell them, 'I ain't got no secret.'"

Then still addressing the cows, he proceeded to tell the secret. Plow the ground deep. Watermelons need more air than water, and deep plowing lets in air.

"I plow turrible deep. Eight or ten inches." He grinned with private satisfaction and moved on to a strawberry patch.

*　　　*　　　*

Mr. Solenberger believes in humus. He produces it by placing mulch between the rows. A liberal politician in Mississippi enjoys a minor reputation as a gardener by mulching with old copies of *The New York Times*.

Mr. Solenberger does not take *The Times*. He uses last year's crab grass.

"Make sure it's rotten," he said, jabbing the air with an open pocketknife for emphasis. "If you plow under something that ain't rotten, it's a detriment to you for the first season."

Many of his neighbors plant by the moon. That is, they wait until the moon is in a certain phase before putting certain seeds into the ground. Planting by the signs of the moon is an ancient agricultural practice.

"Well sir, I don't pay any attention to the moon," Mr. Solenberger said, "and I'll tell you why. I've got a neighbor that plants by the moon, and I asked him a question one day that he couldn't answer.

"I said, 'You plant a seed in dry ground, when the moon is right, and it won't come up. Then ten days later it comes a rain and that seed sprouts and comes up. But by then the sign of the moon is wrong. How do you account for that?'

"He couldn't answer that. I don't plant by the moon. I plant by the ground."

*   *   *

However, Mr. Solenberger and many others in this area share a belief that the weather is undergoing a basic and mysterious change. He is a little troubled by the frosts that seem to come later each spring, just as the force that drives him to the plow seems to have arrived late this year.

"The timber's awful slow a-leafing out," he said, casting a blue eye toward the hill across the road. "When I was a boy, we weren't bothered with frost. When spring come, it come. Our spring's almost a month later than it used to be."

He was asked why he thought that was true. He glanced at the visitor's face to see whether the visitor was ready to accept what he had to say.

"Well sir," he replied, "I believe the world twists a little bit. You know, everything that grows twists around to the right. Follows the sun. Even our storms that come out of the Gulf, they twist to the right. It's just nature."

*   *   *

Why is a man of 86 years still involved every April with the earth's greening, as if it were his own? He passed the question off quickly.

"I just like to be doing things," he said, indicating that it was merely the same motive that led him to do card tricks and tell jokes and graft tomatoes to poke weed.

But he returned to it later, in a round-about way. He confessed that spring was his favorite season.

"Life is at a high ebb in the spring," he said. "People who are getting up in years, more of them die in the winter when the days are short, and in the hours after midnight. Life is at a low ebb after midnight and in the short days. Did you know that? And the shorter the days, the lower the ebb is."

Thus, it is the lengthening days that send Ira Solenberger to the garden, and he can no more resist that than the hapless oak bud can resist becoming a leaf.

Editor's note: Ira Solenberger died December 18, 1977. Death finally got him in the winter, when he was at a low ebb.

Cats, Cattle, and People—

Beware of Dog Days

Hogeye, Ark., July 28, 1975—Seth Timmons reports that he did not sleep well the other night because of a katydid that sang outside his window all night long after the others had stopped.

Not only that, he says, he has been unable to get his work done lately, for no apparent reason. He believes that he is fortunate to have gotten his hay in, considering the way things have been going.

He is not alone in his condition. For days, the cattle have passed the afternoons huddled motionless in the shade. The cats have lain on the steps in perfect imitation of death and have had to be kicked out of the way by every person going through the door.

The cats, the cattle, and Mr. Timmons are all apparently beset by the same affliction. They are in the clutches of the dog days. This is the time when evil is on the land, when dogs and snakes must be watched with special care and when all living things seem to wilt under some baleful influence.

It is the time when people, even sound and mild-tempered men like Seth Timmons, are likely to become fretful and out of kilter.

In the city, dog days have come to mean little more than an ill-defined period of heat and lassitude. They have a sharper meaning in the country, especially in the rural South, where the ancient ideas that were conceived in nature linger with special strength.

The dog days are those that either precede or follow—depending on varying calculations and theories—the time when the dog star, Sirius, begins to rise with the sun. Most almanacs say they begin July 3 and end August 11.

"Noted from ancient times as the hottest and most unwholesome period of the year," says the *Oxford English Dictionary*, and many rural people would agree.

The coming of dog days is marked by a number of natural

changes in the country. The flies increase and cattle get pink-eye. Rain becomes scarce.

Many gardens here in the Ozark Mountains have withered in the heat during the last two weeks. When a light shower does fall, infrequently, its main effect is to revive the ticks and chiggers.

The urgent, lonesome call of the whip-poor-will is no longer heard at night, except occasionally just before dawn and far back in the woods. The dominant night sounds have become the tuneless songs of the katydids, the tree frogs, and the crickets, messengers of ennui and discontent.

In the daytime, the bobwhites and the meadowlarks have practically fallen silent and the fields are left to the bickering crows.

Nadine Findahl, who grew up in rural Minnesota and now lives on a farm here, recalls that Minnesota children were forbidden to swim in the lakes and streams during dog days because the water was stagnant and believed to be unhealthy. That is also a common belief in the South, and one that is commonly defied by the young.

Since the dog days began, it has been so dry here that the children have had difficulty finding a swimming hole full enough to swim in.

As might be expected, the rural creatures that have the most to fear from dog days are the dogs. There is an old country theory that this is the time when dogs are most likely to get rabies.

"When I was a boy growing up in South Arkansas," Ernie Deane, a newspaperman and teacher at nearby Fayetteville, said the other day, "we were told to leave the stray dogs alone during dog days, and, as a matter of fact, to beware of dogs in general, because that was the time they were supposed to go mad.

"I never heard the word 'rabies' until I was grown. A lot of dogs were killed every summer because people thought they were mad dogs. Any poor dog that had a fit during dog days was probably doomed."

Vance Randolph, an authority on Ozarks folklore, says he has been told of mountain towns that have ordinances requiring people to confine their dogs during dog days.

The connection between the dog star and dogs is obvious enough, but how does one explain the pernicious influence that Sirius is said to exert on snakes? A widespread belief in the Ozarks and elsewhere is that snakes go blind and shed their skins during the dog days. Poisonous snakes like copperheads are especially to be watched for at this time because, being blind, they will strike at any nearby sound.

But even nonpoisonous snakes become unaccountably belligerent during dog days, according to some sources.

In his book, *Ozark Magic and Folklore*, Mr. Randolph writes, "Uncle Israel Bonebreak, an ordinarily reliable old gentleman who lives near Pineville, Mo., tells me that he has often seen black snakes, chicken snakes, milk snakes, and other harmless serpents deliberately attack human beings during the dog day period."

All things considered, it is understandable in a season such as this that a man of so serene a disposition as Seth Timmons, who has heard the katydids replace the whip-poor-wills in the valley every July for 63 years, could be kept awake by a single perverse katydid. It is clear to his neighbors that the gravitational pull of the dog star is working on Seth. And on them all, for that matter.

 **Miller Williams**

The Wall

"Man, you just don't know," John Oscar Carpenter said, passing from the shadows of the gym into the hard sunlight, barely turning to aim the words at Kelvin, standing guard in the doorway. "You don't know what you're missing." And the truth of the matter was just that. Kelvin Fletcher *didn't* know what he was missing. Maybe, if he had, he could have put it out of his mind. If he could have visualized the girls in their underthings, petticoats anyway, if he could have made the picture in his mind, he could have forgotten it. With no skirts on, or maybe less, but not naked—not with nothing on, no matter what John Oscar said. That was too much. Already, thinking about the girls in their small white or pink things, or whatever, it was almost impossible to sleep at night.

But mostly that was because John Oscar was right. Because he couldn't see them. Couldn't make them take shape. He tried to make them walk around the way they must walk on the other side of the wall, not knowing they are being looked at, easy and not embarrassed or conscious of themselves, but they wouldn't stay in place. It was like trying to imagine a dog running, really leg by leg imagine him running. It never looked right. He would try to focus on a girl and she slipped out of shape and spread out and twisted around until she didn't look like a girl anymore or anything at all, with a watermelon bottom and five or six breasts that kept crawling around her chest and belly like turtles.

Kelvin remembered how he used to take the little people shaped out of Kleen Klay at Vacation Bible School and squeeze

Miller Williams was born in Hoxie, Arkansas, April 8, 1930. He is the author of several books, the most recent of which are *Sonnets of Giuseppe Belli*, translations from the Italian, and the sixth volume of his own poems, *Distractions*, both from the LSU Press. He lives with his wife, Jordan, in Fayetteville, where he teaches at the University of Arkansas.

them together into a glob with only colors running through it and signs of heads and legs. That was the way the undressed girls in his mind kept contorting into one another.

John Oscar was right. If he had seen once for himself, if he could call to his mind the shape of one girl—of Selina Mae Becker—standing in front of him—Selina Mae Becker—he could say the way he heard Burnett Holloman who didn't seem to believe it say, "When you've seen one, you've seen 'em all." But he couldn't say that. It wouldn't mean anything, because he hadn't seen one. He couldn't even imagine clearly what the boys looking through the hole in the wall were seeing. The trouble with him, and he knew it, was simply that he didn't know what he was missing.

Clement Long, for instance, who probably could see a girl in his mind like anything never seemed interested in the wall that was this minute not quite stopping the sound of the girls on the other side of it. That might have been because Clement was too dignified. Not too dignified to look, of course, but to go climbing up the pile of tables and chairs and boxes that made the crooked tower leaning at a precarious angle against the partition. The wall divided the old gym into two oversize dressing rooms and in the four months it had been put up most of the boys Kelvin knew had climbed at least once to the top of the tower to brace against the sheetrock almost twenty feet off the floor and look through the hole John Oscar had first thought of making.

During the last period of the day, girls from study hall came to the gym to shoot a few goals or tumble and for a couple of hours after school the girls' basketball team and track team and the tumblers were prancing and jostling in and out of the gym, getting ready for the girls' track meet coming up in a few weeks, or simply making use of the field and equipment the boys monopolized during school hours at their own gym periods. After school the only boys out were football players, and the track and mats and the main basketball court belonged to the girls. Some of them, at any one time—as John Oscar had noticed—were in the dressing room, changing their clothes.

The hole was so small that Kelvin could not see it from where he stood now at the door of the gym, watching for the approach of Coach Eberly. But he knew it was big enough and he knew that through it were seen wonders like nothing he had seen for a nickel at the Penny Arcade where the woman in black veils danced and didn't do anything else and only danced again for another nickel.

Once he had turned the crank a little at a time to see if she would move slowly and he could get used to her but she only changed from one frozen position to another as the picture cards flipped over. Both the nickels were for church, but he didn't do that often, almost never. There was nothing in it anyway because she was as old as his Sunday School teacher at least and because he was still saved then and was always afraid when he sinned. Afraid because he knew that his father even if he wasn't a preacher was an agent in God's secret service, that he was guided to evil as if he could see across town and through walls.

The only time Kelvin had slipped away from prayer meeting to spend his offering money on a movie he had felt his father's hand fall on his shoulder and it was as if a zombie had left the screen and slipped into the row of seats behind him. The only time he had smoked, when he was eleven, in the tree-house next door, his father had seen him from an upstairs window and the sudden explosion of his voice calling Kelvin's name was too much like thunder from high above the earth for Kelvin ever to forget the fear of God and his people.

Kelvin was not lost now, but he no longer fell much into sin. He walked into it. There was the pinball machine at the drugstore he played now almost every day. Twice he had gone to the show on Sunday. Yesterday he had told a dirty joke and listened to a better one. The thing was that you couldn't find out a lot of things without sinning and couldn't be much with anybody but God and finally that wasn't enough anymore. He wasn't saved, but he knew what sin was and he still believed in it and the thing was that he knew when he was sinning and didn't try to make it all right by explaining why it wasn't a sin the way Burnett Holloman always did.

He wondered sometimes if God like his father forgives you if you don't lie about what you did and admit it. He decided mostly when he thought about it that you still go to hell.

It was not God who had changed.

"Hey, Kelvin!" Russell Goode said, stopping at the gym door and shifting a load of books in the crook of his arm. "C'mon let's get a Coke."

"I can't," Kelvin said. "I'm watching."

"Did you get a turn?"

"No," Kelvin said, in the same matter-of-fact voice. "Seen one you've seen 'em all."

"And that's a crock of shit, too," Russell said, shifting his books again. "You ain't seen 'em all till you've seen 'em all."

Kelvin meant to smile but it didn't straighten out right.

"Go on, grab a look," Russell said, moving into the shadow of the doorway. "I'll watch out for you."

"No, I can't. I told John Oscar I wouldn't go anywhere till he came back by."

"You're scared."

Kelvin shrugged and Russell Goode hefted his books again.

"I'm not exactly scared," Kelvin mumbled, almost too low to be heard.

"Then get on in there. Ain't nothin' to worry about."

Kelvin looked at the tower and the boy on his knees high above them, looking into another world. He could feel his face flush and he was aware of his heart beating.

"Sure there's something to worry about," he said, turning his eyes back to brightness outside.

A red book dropped from under Russell's arm and Kelvin watched him pick it up as he talked. "Shit, Kelvin. Ain't a thing in the world can happen as long as somebody stays on the door."

"That's what *you* say."

"Well, what then?"

"I don't know," Kelvin said. "But sure as peedunk I'd get caught."

"How come?"

"Russell, you don't *know* me. I *always* get caught."

Ten minutes later John Oscar showed up.

"It's about time you got here," Kelvin said, jumping up from the squat he had dropped to when Russell left. His legs hurt when he straightened them and his right foot was asleep. "Gosh damn! I'll never make it home."

"What's the matter? It's not even four."

"I got to get my homework before supper. It's Wednesday night."

"Hell," John Oscar said, "what's Wednesday night?"

"Hell, stupid. Prayer meeting is Wednesday. Don't you know anything?"

"You have to go to *that*?"

Kelvin was supporting himself on his left leg, leaning against the building and holding his right foot suspended so that it could come to as painlessly as possible.

"It's not so bad. Anyway, I don't guess it's going to hurt me," and he let his foot down and hobbled off, following the shadow of the school building, walking more naturally after the first few yards, then kicking stones aside, watching them roll and bounce out of his path. When he turned suddenly around the corner of the building, out of John Oscar's sight, he broke into a hard run.

*   *   *

His father was reading the newspaper and didn't look up. "You're late. School's been out an hour."

It hadn't been out that long, but Kelvin knew not to argue the point. He had fashioned his lie before he had run three blocks, and it came out easily. "Miss Verckle kept us to work on something. If we wanted to. You get extra credit."

"On what?" Paul Fletcher turned a page of the paper and folded it around with a snap of his long heavy arms. He creased it and laid it in his lap and then he turned and looked at Kelvin leaning back against the front door, breathing heavily, his face redder than usual. Kelvin's right arm was bent behind him where his hand still clung tightly to the brass knob. "What were you working on?"

"For an assembly program. For Government."

"That going to help your grade?"

"It's extra credit."

"Well, you're going to need extra credit if you don't get your homework. Did you forget this is Wednesday night?"

"No sir, I remembered. I ran all the way home."

"I see you did. Where are your books?"

"I don't have to use them. All I have to do is practice a talk. And make up some problems for math. I don't need my books." It was a lie.

Kelvin was astonished and proud and ashamed that it had come so readily, with no sign of his own disgust that he had forgotten his books, left them at the gym door.

He would not be able to do his homework now, but it would be better to face his teachers than to anger his father.

"Well, you better get on it," his father said, and turned back to his paper. Kelvin went upstairs to his room and made up math problems until he was called to supper.

*   *   *

At prayer meeting he saw Selina Mae Becker and her mother. During a stand-up hymn he made a tube with his fist and looked through it at Selina Mae. He tried to imagine she was changing clothes but it didn't work. Then Brother Simmons prayed and talked about what prayer is for. Kelvin listened to him and forgot the hole in the wall and the girls. He thought about God and believed that somehow God was thinking about him and before it was time for everybody to make a silent prayer Kelvin closed his ears to Brother Simmons and shut his eyes and prayed. He had moved his lips silently for no more than a few words when he knew God wasn't hearing him.

*   *   *

Later, in bed, he prayed again, and he felt better. He took his Bible from his lamp table and read something about principalities and became sleepy.

He woke up the next morning with the Bible under his face. He was sore where it had pressed against his cheekbone and left an impression on his freckled skin.

*   *   *

It was Thursday, and there was no need to rush home. There was still the Government assembly program to prepare for and there was no prayer meeting. He took the second watch at the gym door. The schoolyard, as much as he could see of it, was deserted, except for now and then a boy cutting across to the drugstore or coming over to wait for a turn at the tower. Kelvin kept his eyes open for any adults or any younger students who couldn't be trusted with the secret, and his ears were full always of the sounds of the four-man basketball game that went on whenever there was anyone on the tower. It was an excuse for the boys' presence in the gym after school every day, and they hoped too that it would make less noticeable the unavoidable sounds of tower-climbing that might carry over onto the girls' side.

When he was relieved, a little after four, he didn't go home. He stepped inside the gym and watched the ball game for a few minutes and then he joined it and played until he heard a high laugh from the other side of the wall and gave up the ball and quit pretending. There were only two boys waiting at the tower and he got in line behind them. They were only allowed two minutes apiece if anyone was waiting, and Kelvin hoped someone would come behind him so that he would be forced to come down right away. Visions were swimming in his head, visions of himself freezing at the top of the tower, visions of being struck blind for looking. He knew that one quick look would be enough. He wanted to go up and to come down, with as little time between as possible.

The climb was not as easy as he had thought it would be. Nothing but gravity held the pieces of the tower together and he wasn't sure gravity was going to be enough. Jaybo West and Earl Dean Johnson helped him up and Harvey Lee Simpson the preacher's son steadied the furniture as well as he could, counter-balancing Kelvin's weight with his own until his hands couldn't reach anymore. Twice Kelvin thought he was falling.

"Look out, stupid!" Earl Dean shouted in a whisper. "You're going to knock it over!"

Kelvin didn't breathe until the tower swayed slowly back into place. Behind the school he could hear the band practicing for Saturday's football game. He knew that in a little while they would be marching around the building and past the gym door. He started to climb down but he knew the boys would not forgive him for that, once he had started up.

It was not difficult to balance, after you got to the top. Kneeling on the plank that lay over the large box on the table supported by the chairs that stood each on a box on a chair, he could lean forward comfortably with his hands and head braced against the wall and with his right eye precisely over the hole. The hole was so large now that he was afraid at first one of the girls would surely see it. But they never had and they wouldn't.

It took a second for the sight to register, then when it did he thought his heart would throw him down to the floor. *Oh God Jesus don't let anyone else get in line.*

The first thing was that some of the girls were sure enough naked. Three. Annette Freeman and Betty Sue House and a girl whose name he could never remember. He hated himself for not being able to remember it now. The second thing was that almost everybody was standing and walking and laughing and talking the way boys do and he wondered if someone was going to pop someone's bottom with a towel. The third thing was Miss King the gym teacher in white shorts and white tennis shoes and taking her shirt off. The fourth thing was that Selina Mae Becker was not there. The fifth thing was that he had a hard on and he had to squeeze his legs together or something but he knew that if he did he might fall. He heard the band marching past on its first circle around the building, stepping to fast drums.

Betty Sue House took a towel from a wooden bench and threw it over her shoulder and walked toward the shower stalls out of Kelvin's line of vision to his left. He noticed that her breasts were smaller than he had thought they would be. When she had disappeared he turned his eye back to Annette Freeman and saw with a strange delight that her breasts were larger than they had ever seemed and his single eye followed their rhythm as she followed Betty Sue's path toward the showers. Most of the girls were still in their white shorts and shirts, and some already had showered and had their slips or dresses on or were getting into and out of things. Kelvin looked with slow long looks at long legs and navels and bright red nipples on soft tits that didn't crawl like turtles. He knew that if he didn't get down he was going to burst. He heard the band coming around the building again, all horns now, playing something loud and full of spirit.

Suddenly he felt dizzy. The tower seemed to sway to the right and then to the left and he looked down and saw that it was not him but the tower itself. Jaybo and Harvey Lee were doing their desperate best to right it and Earl Dean was holding his hands up as if he could calm it down the way a teacher shuts up a classroom of children. Kelvin leaned gently against the wall and tried to brace himself and the tower together. The wood made a scraping noise against the sheetrock and Kelvin pushed the top of the tower out an inch from the wall. The band came closer, so close that Kelvin thought it was going to march straight in through the gym door and up to the wall but they turned and filed smartly past, trumpets playing alone, playing a wild music no man ever wrote.

Then the wall gave way. Slowly at first, leaning over toward the girls, bulging with Kelvin's weight. Then to each side of him the wall cracked, leaving a large center section to lean far out over the dressed and half dressed and undressed girls, running back from it, standing aghast, covering themselves with hands and towels. Kelvin looked back in terror to see the rear ends of three blue jeans, one white shirt tail flying, fade into the sunlight. The corner of his eye caught the abandoned basketball still rolling across the floor. The tower held now, leaning and falling with the broken section, and kept him from sliding down the slanting wall and running on broken ankles after his friends.

Then the wall fell and Kelvin rode it down. There was a whoosh of air rushing from beneath it. He heard a girl scream and in the distance he heard marching music.

The last thing he saw of the world zooming toward him was a long bare arm with a finger pointing at a boy falling out of the sky. Then he hit and there were explosions of pain in his knees. The first thing he saw when the nausea passed was someone not himself on all fours in the middle of the girls' dressing room, his face still centered over the gigantic hole in the sheetrock as the gym teacher, in white shorts and white tennis shoes and sox and nothing else at all beat him viciously over the head with a towel. The teacher was making sounds Kelvin couldn't understand and in her eyes there was a look of more than rage. She held the towel like a club in both hands and swung it again and again at the motionless unbelievable head. Two shapes hid behind her and vaguely to his right what was left of Rosemary Rutledge crouched down, her chin between her knees, eyes and mouth wide open and locked, her panties clutched forgotten in her white fist.

The room turned over and there was no one left but the teacher and the boy and Rosemary. Miss King swept the room with her eyes and screamed at the girl. "Get out of here, you little idiot! Get the hell out of here and get your clothes on!"

Then there was no one left but the teacher and the boy, and gradually Kelvin Fletcher knew who the boy was.

The principal had gone home but the teacher telephoned him. As Kelvin waited with her in the office where still she spoke not a single word to him, he thought of the two things that took over his mind. That now Selina Mae Becker would never want him, and that it didn't matter anyway because his father was maybe going to kill him and if his father didn't, he would do it himself.

"I told you, Goddam!" he screamed in his mind at Russell

Goode and all the legs disappearing into the sun. "I told you I always get caught!"

Already he could feel the powerful grip of his father's hand on his shoulders. He looked at the rough grain of the desk and the patterns in the tile floor and knew that his father would not kill him and that he would not kill himself either and the question now, since he would have to live through it and since there was no choice but to tell the truth, was how much his father would understand about sin.

 **William Harrison**

Down the Blue Hole

This mystic arcadian village is called Poplar Bluff, Missouri, and, sure, you've heard of it, but you probably never knew that every day we have dozens of seances, prophecies by seers and visionaries, and the assorted practice of witches, astrologers, magicians, and even, perhaps, one ghoul.

This is the little town where I live, though I've thought of moving away because of all the competition. The pressure to exceed one's best effort is so awful here that I've considered moving up to St. Louis and losing myself in the mercenary and nonpsychic life.

For instance, the other night I had sixteen snickering tourists at my table, sitting in a circle with their hands extended and palms upright, lights out, and the thunder cracked and everybody jumped and screamed, their index fingers pricked so that a single drop of blood blossomed on each one. When I switched on the lights there they were, astounded—they all admitted it. And I blotted each finger with a Kleenex and put all the bloody tissues into my big glass cookie jar and told them wild stories about how I would mingle their blood and put them under a spell. They gasped and laughed and loved it. One of them asked how I ever did such a trick. Then they started talking about old Auntie Sybil, one of my competitors, and the whole effect dissolved.

Someone else wanted to know if I served refreshments.

William Harrison was born in 1933 in Dallas, Texas. For the last fifteen years he has taught at the University of Arkansas, where he founded the graduate writing program. He has written five novels; among them are *In a Wild Sanctuary* (1970) and *Africana* (1977), a collection of short stories and a number of screenplays that includes *Rollerball*. His stories, articles, and reviews have appeared in *Esquire*, *Harper's*, *Playboy*, *Paris Review*, *Travel & Leisure*, and other magazines. Currently he is at work on a long historical novel, *Burton and Speke*, his third novel set in Africa.

*   *   *

My biggest act is my disappearing act where I just vanish. I go off into the Blue Hole, don't ask me how.

I've done this trick six times now: sit cross-legged under my velvet cloth, concentrate, melt my bones and my whole petty life into nothing, while the audience watches that cloth sag and empty itself. It's a great act because it's no act at all; off in the limbo of the Blue Hole I'm frightened, naturally, but I come back every time. Once I did this at the annual Rotary Banquet, vanishing under my velvet cloth at the rear of the hall, then coming up underneath the tablecloth beside the main speaker, rattling spoons and spilling ham loaf onto the floor, rising like Vesuvius forty feet from the spot where I disappeared. They were so pleased that they gave me an extra $25 and asked me back next year.

This is such a forlorn life for a great talent.

*   *   *

Funk and Wagnall's Encyclopedia describes our part of the state as flat and alluvial. Sort of dull, right: this is an agricultural stop, a market town for cotton and soybeans, a town with only a few important ranchers and a nice high school.

True, Mrs. Marybush, the town matron and benefactor, dresses like one of the key figures from the Tarot deck. Also, we have some housewives who give the evil eye to the butchers and the boys at the check-out counters at Krogers —where one can sometimes detect a slight levitation in the vegetable scale.

How this place happened I don't know. When I came here years ago there were just a few spiritualists and a couple of horoscope addicts. I was just a country boy from over in Stoddard County, town of Zeta, and Poplar Bluff, I felt, had a ready audience for what I already reckoned was my considerable talent. Yet this town has become a kind of curse: tourists pour in all year, strangers all, there are loonies and charlatans everywhere, and the pressure, as I said, on one's craft is enormous.

Tourists are so unappreciative, too. One night I was making excellent contact with the dead at my table, summoning up a clear apparition, and this farmer recognizes the face and drawls, "Uncle Pardue, hey! This here is Bobby Wayne!

Where'd you put that gold watch and fob you promised you'd leave me? We can't find that baby nowhere!"

Just as Las Vegas has its slot machines in the supermarkets, so our town exposes its soul in public; we have tea-leaf readers in every dumpy café, newsstands with astrological charts and no news, and one famous washer-woman—Auntie Sybil, yes—who advertises bona fide trances while she does up your clothes. In truth, Auntie Sybil's act is pretty good; she lives in a simple clapboard house on the edge of town, so a customer can drive out there with his bundle of wash and hear all the dire and wonderful predictions for his future while Auntie Sybil works. She's an old bag, about ninety, and very authentic. There with the Borax, her ironing board set up in her steamy kitchen, running your underwear through her old Maytag wringer, she communicates with the cosmos in your behalf. Also, voices from the past come straight out of her throat while she's in a trance—you pay $5 extra for this. She does a terrific Caesar Augustus and a good Mahatma Gandhi.

*   *   *

My name is Homer Bogardus, though after I left Stoddard County I dropped the first name altogether and my sign out front now reads Mr. Mystic, and, in smaller letters underneath, The Great Bogardus. This house of turrets, broad eaves and Gothic hallways is my castle and dismay—a pox, dammit, on the plumbing.

My memory of my early real world is dim and colorless, and, as I say about that, good riddance. Women, money, plumbing, friends: every reality I ever met addled and confounded me. The town of Zeta, symbolic in its very name of last things, almost ended me, true enough, and I used to contemplate mutilation and suicide in that cupboard of an upstairs room in Daddy's farmhouse. I might have been an idiot child chained to an iron bedstead and thrown crusts of bread, for it was that bad: I felt my adolescence like a disease, I pined, I bit my knuckles with anguish. One day—this was after hearing about Poplar Bluff and the lure of its underground—I fell into concentration and poured myself a glass of water from the pewter pitcher on the bureau although I sat twenty feet across my room in the window seat where I gazed out over Daddy's fields. I extended my physical powers across space and moved the pitcher and floated a brimming glass of water into my hands. Ninety magic days later I packed my bag and came in search of destiny.

Life before that, in all its lousy reality, was a wound. A strapping neighbor girl, Helen Rae, invited me into her barn, once, then successfully fought me off, breaking my collarbone in the fracas. My best buddy, Elroy, sabotaged my 4-H project for no reason at all. And Daddy died, to spite me for being different, I thought at the time—though in a seance, since, he materialized and denied it. And we were helplessly poor: cardboard innersoles in my dismal brogans.

So I left everything and hitchhiked to Poplar Bluff and the closets of my head.

What's so good about reality anyway? My bills are still mostly unpaid, my colleagues consider me odd in a town of oddities, my plumbing groans, my love life is asunder. Some days, like today, I dream beyond my powers—what if I *can* do almost anything?—to the Blue Hole where it might not be so bad to live forever.

*   *   *

"Produce a girl for me, a true love," I beg Auntie Sybil.

We're sitting in her famous kitchen while she makes lye soap. A Hollywood game show screams from her portable.

"You're unlucky in love," she offers.

"Don't give me that old line. I need what I need."

She fixes me with those depthless eyes; all mystery is behind those black slits, all knowledge, the dream of dreams. "All right, for fifty dollars cold cash I'll give it one hell of a try," she says.

"Conjure hard," I plead, peeling off the bills. "And for this price, please, I ought to get some fast action."

"You shouldn't even dally with the flesh, Bogardus," she tells me, putting my money under the radio. "You possess a great talent, enough for anyone to live for. If you had any talent for promotion, you could get on television."

That night a miracle enters my house. Sally Ritchie is a local girl back home from college, a strange, lovely spirit—incidentally thin of waist and ample of bosom—who has come, she says, in search of my netherworld. Her heart, she adds, has been broken by an athlete.

"Give me some sign," she breathes.

"I certainly will," I tell her, and I show her my collection of

Oriental bells with no clappers. Then we sit holding hands in my parlor while I make them vibrate and ring.

"My god," Sally Ritchie breathes more heavily. "You are *good!*"

*   *   *

Though I'm trying to be in love and loved again, the town goes on as usual. In the church the minister begins his sermon and then begins to cry, as if possessed, a Black Mass.

Our postman, Mr. Denbo, refuses to deliver any more packages to the Cabal Institute because, he says, there are live things inside.

At the annual cakewalk some hippie warlocks and vampiresses appear, but Mayor Watson strolls across the gymnasium to reason with them.

"We don't want your kind here," he explains.

One of the kids gets sassy and gives the mayor some vulgar lip. "Decay," he says to the mayor. "Palsy. Extreme. Burp. Bloat. Pimple. Gronk. Kidney. Suck. Waddle."

*   *   *

Sally Ritchie contends that she adores me, but clearly she craves only the sensation of my powers; ever since I told her that I'm capable of complete dematerialization she has pleaded and insisted.

"Love me, not my talent," I ask of her, but she claims this is psychologically impossible. Her college boyfriend, the one who jilted her, played guard on the basketball team, she points out, and she adored his dribble.

She attends my nightly gatherings, applauding each wonder.

Tonight a dozen tourists receive a superior set of hallucinations: my old reptile-and-animal special. Encircling my table, hands touching, they sit and witness the ghostly albino Great Dane who moves through the room, passes into walls, emerges again. We detect his panting breath as he haunts us. This beast, I explain, and I tell them the absolute truth, has been a resident of this house for years, long before I came here; he is terribly restless. Harmless pet, no problem, I assure everyone, and they tilt first one way and then another—feel the pull of my fingers, Sally?—to glimpse him padding around.

Then the snakes: I move them into the room and have them

slither across our shoes beneath the table. Hands tighten. Audible gasps. But this is just the frightening beginning; soon the serpents are coiling up and over us, a net of white underbellies over our arms and shoulders, and only my soothing voice prevents absolute hysteria.

The table is a writhing pit: black and green snakes everywhere. And now a thick furry adder: it rises among them like a sentinel, one large eye in the middle of its head, and I say, "Look at that eye, ladies and gentlemen, each one of you look into that eye!"

The one-eyed adder stops before each participant and stares him down. Meanwhile, the other serpents curl away and vanish — and the big one is gone, too, and the evening is a triumph.

"I could do my giant spider now," I tentatively offer.

"Oh, no, no, don't bother," everyone assures me.

"Wonderful," Sally Ritchie breathes. "And it was your eye in there, wasn't it, Mr. Bogardus? It was your eye inside that big snake, right?"

*   *   *

Deep in the Blue Hole.

I am here because Sally Ritchie wants a thrill.

The hole is like a cave, an indigo cavern, a gigantic drain which spirals down into the basements of the earth. Not so awful in here, really, after a time, so I sit here deciding exactly where I should now emerge. Should it be there in the parlor where I disappeared from Sally's side? No, I decide to make Sally suffer. I shall arise in the garden, calling and beckoning her outdoors so that she will find me bursting through the ground like a weird pod among all the dying autumnal stalks. A splendid gesture, true, so that's exactly how I do it: clods falling off my shoulders as I rise up, a primordial flower sprouting before her very eyes.

It occurs to me as I emerge that I'm trying to earn adoration.

"Forty minutes!" she breathes. "You were gone forty *minutes!* And look at you! Coming up through the *dirt!*"

"A new record," I observe. "Forty minutes in the Blue Hole."

*   *   *

The town ghoul, whose name is Ralph, is generally popular, but I find him morbid. He throws parties after which he tries to get Sally and her girl friends to stay late and go skipping around graveyards, but thank goodness they don't go for that sort of thing. I like Ralph well enough personally, but his art and mine are at odds; he tends to press reality home while I just want to divert and delight. Oh, I throw a few harmless scares into the tourists, sure, but why face them with war, pestilence, and man's cruel heart?

Ralph, like most people, can be somewhat deciphered by his rooms. I slip away from one of his cocktail parties at the Christmas season and tour his house, finding on the tables of his den and bedrooms stuffed hawks, daggers, a dusty crystal ball, and ashtrays made of old manacles. His bedroom is a gray, dim dungeon of a place.

A few days later, still thinking about rooms, I decide to indulge in a little astral flight and visit my Sally's bedroom. She has the upstairs of her parents' big Georgian over on Maple Avenue.

I watch her sleeping, a brown shower of her lovely hair across the pillow.

Soon, I learn she is returning to school.

Do you want subtleties from me? The difference between my astral travels and complete dematerialization? All my mind-over-matter conquests explained? Do you want me to tell you why I'm so frivolous, why I don't use my powers to cure sickness, or, like that flashy French clairvoyant, fight crime and evil? Why should I compound my despair with endless explanation? What do you need except moments of profound awe?

*   *   *

Sally Ritchie writes that she is flunking biology.

It is darkest January and the Ozarks are blanketed in snow; at my window I can hear the world creaking beneath its ice, swaying and moaning in the winter thrall. The plumbing in my house answers noises.

I read my own palm and what do I see there? A private landscape as bleak as Poplar Bluff: a powerful life that can do all things, but is leaking away.

Accepting Ralph's invitation, I go over and catch the Super Bowl game on his crystal ball—nice reception, few ghosts, no commercials. We sit close at the table in his den, sipping cognacs, and staring into that small glass dream. Ralph, who is becoming morosely drunk, twitches his mustache and leers at me occasionally, but I don't mind.

"Thanks for asking me over," I tell him, and mean it.

*   *   *

In February I consider the Mardi Gras in New Orleans, the Acropolis, Kaanapali Beach in Hawaii, Marbella: all those vacation spots where I could go in an instant, where I could amaze the jet sets, charge supernatural fees, and forget Sally Ritchie and all the wretched consequences of my talents.

Instead, on the icy street outside the drugstore—Valentine in hand, yes, ready for mailing—I draw my cape around me and tip my hat to Mrs. Marybush, who, today, is dressed like the Hanged Man. She smiles at my courtesy and informs me that she is sending friends from Kansas City to my table—skeptics, all, who need a good lesson.

"I'm not interested in the conversion of the masses," I snap at poor Mrs. Marybush. "Nor in offering proofs. Nor in metaphysical debate. I'm not going to call the lightning from the skies for another roomful of hicks. In fact, I'm retiring."

"No need to get huffy, Mr. Bogardus," she answers, and turns with her nose high and walks away.

*   *   *

In the spring there are county fairs, two of them, at Poplar Bluff and at Cape Girardeau more than fifty miles away, and I contract to perform my supreme act at them both—simultaneously.

The fair at Cape Girardeau is one of cheap tinsel and wheezing merry-go-rounds with all the splendor and illusion of a ghetto, yet the fairgrounds border the mighty Mississippi River, swollen with our winter rains, majestic, the elms and poplars on its banks rattling with extraordinary music.

All the people of my life mill around in the sunlit crowd: Daddy, Mr. Denbo, Auntie Sybil, Elroy, Mayor Watson, Helen Rae, Ralph, Mrs. Marybush, Sally Ritchie, and hundreds I haven't told you about.

Odors of mustard and cotton candy assail us. The television crew hurries around and the director, a sallow young man with a gold tooth, regards me with doubt—although the president of the Poplar Bluff Rotary Club has given assurances that this will absolutely come off as guaranteed. I eat a candied apple and gaze into the sky. A chilly day in April.

The cirrus clouds streak overhead, the pulse of the river is in us all, beating in our blood beneath the hurdy-gurdy sounds of the carnival; today I will melt away under my velvet canopy, I will enter the endless cavern of the Blue Hole, and rise again in Poplar Bluff, miles away, while two sets of cameras record the miracle.

A reporter from the *Post-Dispatch* interviews my colleagues, all of whom are here to bask in the fallout of publicity. There is Auntie Sybil, true to her down-home image, peddling a basket of lye soap and preserves among the crowd. That simple country crone. As Mrs. Marybush and the mayor sign up tourist business for the forthcoming seances, Ralph tells a reporter that "Poplar Bluff is the mysterious metaphor of America"—a phrase which the reporter scribbles in a small spiral notebook.

"You'll meet someone else," Sally Ritchie tells me as we lurk by a sideshow tent. "You have a lot to give."

Faced with Sally's clichés, I'm tempted to ask her to join me, to disappear with me this afternoon under the velvet—she's such a fool for all the hoopla and drumroll.

She wears an oversized letter sweater, oxfords, a ribbon in her hair. "I'll be proud," she goes on, "to say that I once knew you, Mr. Bogardus." She squeezes my hand, the only way she has ever touched me.

As I mount the stage, cameras whirring, the river glistening beyond the trees, a chilly breeze billowing up under my cape, I think of my house. Not too far away, there it stands: all boarded up at last, my sign removed, the furniture draped and covered in each room, chairs turned upside down on the great table where my powers ruled. I can visualize inevitable details: my kitchen faucet still dripping.

Will the Great Dane remain there, I wonder, to haunt the dust of those rooms? Will my absence be interpreted as failure or as just a mighty one-way effort into the unknown? Will this negate all the sad wonders of my life? Or will societies and scholars come to study me, to peruse my insurance policy and read the marginalia in my volumes? Will they seek to retrieve me in future seances? Or ask Sally Ritchie to recollect, to salvage memories and anecdotes?

The Cape Girardeau High School band plays "Columbia, the Gem of the Ocean," and down I go, I melt, going away, all gone, never to explain myself or my miracles again, not even these words that vanish now—poof!—upon this mysterious page.

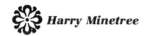 **Harry Minetree**

The Current Revisited

Not long ago a New York actor friend who delights in the fact that I'm from a small town with a colorful name, introduced me to Stewart Udall, who was Secretary of the Department of the Interior under John Kennedy. "Minetree's from Poplar Bluff, Missouri!" the actor said with a condescending smile. "Really?" Udall replied. "Did you know Doc Stokely?"

"As a matter of fact," I said, glancing at the actor, "he taught me how to hunt and fish." The revenge was sweet, but the conversation with Udall was more important.

"If I am remembered by the American people, it will be because of the trip I took to southeast Missouri in 1961 and the Scenic Rivers legislation that came out of it. That's when I met Doc Stokely," Udall continued, "and Len Hall. We floated the Current River, and they convinced me that it had to be saved."

Udall went on to tell how Stokely, the late outdoor columnist for the St. Louis *Post-Dispatch*, and Len Hall, his counter-

Harry Minetree was born April 7, 1935, and grew up in Poplar Bluff, Missouri. He writes:

"I went to school there when I wasn't hunting or fishing—and at Vanderbilt, where I came under the influence of Donald Davidson. I spent a term at Harvard, studying with Allen Tate and Robert Lowell, who were on loan. Then I went to the Iowa Writers Workshop. I taught for seven years, sleeping through faculty meetings and publishing short stories in literary quarterlies.

"I am a sixth-generation Missourian on my mother's side (my father was from Arkansas). One great-grandfather fought for the Confederacy; the other fought for the Union and was a signer of the Missouri Emancipation Proclamation. Both were from Laclede County."

Minetree's works include the biography, *Cooley: The Career of a Great Heart Surgeon* (Harpers, 1973) and all manner of pieces in magazines from *Family Circle* to *Penthouse*. He was nominated for the Overseas Press Club's Hemingway Award for International Journalism. He is currently working on two novels, one set in the Ozarks and one set in Africa.

part at the St. Louis *Globe-Democrat*, had arranged the float trip as a dramatization of what would be lost if the ecological devastation of the area continued. Udall assumed I knew the specifics of that ecological devastation and did not labor details. But like most locals, I was not a student of the land and rivers on which I had been reared, and even now I harbor a vestigal suspicion of outsiders who come to what was once my country and announce the imminence of doom.

My 20-year-old memories of the Current and the rest of those spring-fed Ozark rivers were all good—salad years and swift water. Even the icy capsizings, the sheared pins and snakebites seemed not unpleasant through the haze of years. As Udall spoke, I daydreamed scenes of my early life in the Ozarks—a private stock of images that sustained me as I lost a record salmon on a stream in Cornwall, collapsed of heat prostration during an elephant hunt in the Sudan, or missed whatever I was after on the velds and waters of several continents.

That same evening I phoned Davis Brookreson, a childhood friend back in Poplar Bluff, and arranged a Current River float trip to recapture some of the good old days, so I thought. But what happened was not exactly what I had anticipated.

The day after I arrived via the new airline service to Poplar Bluff, Davis and I packed his four-wheel drive and headed northwest toward the hills. He had lost a tuft or two of hair and had developed a prosperous belly over the years, but otherwise had changed little. Davis is a doctor now, a house-call country sort in the mold of his father and grandfather. He had always loved the woods. And if gear is any index to the expertise of a fisherman, with his Orvis tackle, his Yellow Dog Stetson and those armadillo boots (as kids we had been outfitted by Western Auto), Davis was a top contender for the smallmouth bass crown.

An hour later, after filling the boxes with ice at Bales' Store, we pulled out of Eminence and I could smell the river country. The images came thick and fast: "Do you remember when we put in at Van Buren in that duckboat of Dutch Wyatt's? I smelled like fish for a week!" Davis nodded. "Or that woman," I said. "The one who called us in for sucker and cornbread. We had some string of smallmouths that day! Remember?" He nodded again. "And what about the trip down from Montauk? That big mixed bag of trout and goggle-eye and smallmouth

. . .huh?" Davis smiled. Well, he floated the river several times a year. I couldn't expect him to be as enthusiastic as I was. Then we arrived at Powder Mill Ferry where we had arranged to meet the guides. But they weren't there and neither was the ferry!

"What happened?" I asked. The gravel slope where cars and wagons had boarded was still there, but the current-propelled barge and the snuff-stained old geezer who had run it were gone. "There's a bridge upstream," Davis said. "A lot of things have changed since those big stringers of smallmouths you remember so well!" Before I could respond, two pickups arrived. "Gaylon and the boys," Davis said.

Gaylon Watson—outfitter, guide, high school biology teacher—shook hands, remarked on the lovely day and set to work with the boys, securing balanced loads in three canoes. Jackie Jackson, 83, bent but tough as a pine knot, played strawboss to Gaylon's foreman. "The boys" were Vestor Speck Lewis, soft-spoken and the best fry cook on the river, and Jackie's son Gene, a tall, lean, yarn-spinning veteran of the South Pacific who never left the woods after the war. "Poor?" says Gene.

"You ever try to heat a three-room shack with an electric blanket? Without no electric?"

Since we were late getting started, Gaylon suggested that we forget fishing for the afternoon and try to make the run to the Ant Hole sandbar before dark. "I'm giving you Jackie," Gaylon said, as though assigning a racehorse to a jockey. "He's guided on this river for 60-odd years." "Pop," Gene drawled. "Now don't you go to sleep at the wheel and drownd this feller!" Jackie danced a little jig, did a sort of Queen Anne salute with the boat paddle, then smiled: not a tooth in his tilted head.

The river was even more beautiful than I had remembered—cold and clear as the air. Running to every shade of green and blue, it was mottled in the shallows, white lace in the rapids, and when the angle was right along the smooth, wide chutes, it mirrored the sky and the thick green woods on the hills.

We were in the lead and Jackie, his cap cocked on the side of his head, sang most of the way nameless, tuneless ditties and laments that nonetheless were recognizably pure Ozark. He applauded himself, aping one or another of his seven sons—"Haw, haw, Pop! Now ain't that the real McCoy!"—and somewhat disjointedly dwelt on the women he had known and wanted to know better.

And on game: "I said good-bye to the boys down to the Grandin dock and struck out up river to shoot me a deer. Come round the bend and first off it was the prettiest little ten-point buck you ever seen setting there on the hill. Well, sir, I popped him one with the old 7mm and would you believe that rascal dropped stone-dead and slid down the bank right acrost my boat. I paddled back down around the bend to the dock. Speck says to me, 'My god, Jackie, I never heered of no one killing a deer that fast!' 'Well son,' I says, 'hit don't take long to kill one oncet you find him!' Haw haw!" And he broke out in song again.

The light had begun to fail when we landed on the gravel bar at Ant Hole, but now and then a ray of the setting sun cut through the trees behind us and plumbed the deep blue hole beneath the bluff across the river. A few minutes later, it was dark. Because of an early frost there were no insects or frog songs, only the rapids below camp echoing the crackling of the fire Gene had built. Gaylon made beds in the tents while Speck ignited a bottle-gas jet beneath a well-seasoned cauldron of home-rendered lard. "When a match'll light on the surface," he said, "the grease is ready for the meat. Ain't that right, Doc?" Jackie generally gave instructions.

Davis and I settled in chairs beside the fire, a platter of wild elkhorn mushrooms and a Mason jar of home-pickled rough fish between us. "You know," he said, "your memories about the duckboat full of smallmouth, all those stories that you remember as the good old days, were not really so good." And for the next half hour, interrupted only by an empty glass or Jackie's colorful interjections, Davis reviewed a history of the area of which I had been all but unaware.

Before the countryside was devastated by agricultural mismanagement and human pressures, the Current was the best smallmouth stream in America. That was in the late 1800s when Jesse James was working the area. "Jesse James smallmouth," Davis said. "A lean, mean outlaw lunker! But all that changed; now, fortunately, it is changing back again."

Although the southern Ozarks were discovered by Hernando De Soto in the mid-seventeenth century, the first permanent white settlement wasn't established until after the Homestead Act of 1862. The last Indians had been moved out by cancelled treaty in 1836 and the frontiersmen had already destroyed the antelope, elk and buffalo. Still, there were millions of deer and fur-bearing animals in the sparsely populated hills and the rivers were full of fish.

The serious decline of the area started after the Civil War when bushwhackers drove out the more responsible settlers, and hunters and trappers with no knowledge of agriculture took over the land. They overloaded the glades with cattle and goats, killing off the most nutritious grasses and the young trees. They established one of the largest timber industries in the world, leveling the woods in the watershed, loosening the topsoil and filling the streams with gravel. When the timber was gone, the mills closed, leaving a large population of sawyers and lumberjacks to ravish the land further for a meager subsistence. Under the pressures of dynamiting and uncontrolled gigging, the gamefish population, already stunted by the effects of timbering, declined to near extinction.

The slow recovery began in 1936 when the Missouri government initiated a forestry program; but the big push did not get underway until the mid-60s when the federal government established Jacks Fork, Eleven Point and Current rivers as a Scenic River area. "They are still acquiring land on the rivers," Davis said. "Tearing down cabins, closing free range and controlling the timber-taking. Deer, beaver and turkeys are everywhere. Even the bears are back."

"What about the increased influx of tourists?" I asked.

"Booming. But they're a new breed, ecologically aware conservationists," he said. "There are more people on the river, but they are mostly canoeists who don't fish. They have chased off a lot of the fishermen; consequently fishing is better than it has been in years! As for the lunker smallmouths you remember catching—"

"Soup's on," Speck called. There was lard-fried goggle-eye, wild mushrooms, potatoes, fresh wild greens and beer biscuits, followed by coffee with the consistency and strength of battery acid. After dinner, there was singing and tall-tale telling around the campfire. By midnight everyone had found his cot.

After a big breakfast featuring Speck's infamous 90-weight bacon gravy, we broke camp and headed downriver. During an eight-hour float from Ant Hole to Paint Rock we passed through some of the most spectacular scenery in the country. I did not keep count but would estimate that Davis, Gaylon and I caught and released over 50 keeper smallmouths. That was impressive, even compared with my grand memories of yesteryear, but I was not overwhelmed by the size of the fish.

We had said good-bye to Gaylon and the boys at Paint Rock and were winding our way through the woods when I broached the subject to Davis. "I register it as one of the classic trips. Maybe an all-time high in volume, but none of them were very big like when we were kids."

"Like the ones you remember?" That familiar smile eased across his face. "Well, I remember, too. I was there. Of all the years you and I fished together, our grand total would not match the number of fish we caught today. *One day!* As for size, today's biggest fish would come in at three plus change. That's the *bottom* range of the Jesse James smallmouths that are hiding in the underwater caves these days. The lunkers we caught in 'the good old days' were at best Billy-the-Kids!"

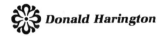 **Donald Harington**

Queen Anne's Lace for Tommie

I

The summer it hurt her to walk, he took her groceries to her, two miles up Swains Creek to her two-room house, once a month, toting on his shoulder a gunny sack filled with a bag of flour, pail of lard, assorted small canned stuff, he thirteen, she past seventy, living alone. She paid him. A quarter in June, fifty cents in July, a dollar in August. Then in September it hurt her not only to walk but also to move, and somebody drove her into Jasper to live with a niece or grandniece, and he never saw her any more, nor did anybody else, not even the family of the niece or grandniece, for it was said that she kept to her room and they put her food on a tray and set it on a chair beside her door and she would get the tray when nobody was looking and eat her food and put the tray back on the chair. When it didn't hurt her too much to move or walk, she would climb out the window and sneak off to the privy; she always refused to use a chamberpot, would not permit one in the same room with her.

It was not until she died and they brought her back to Stay More and buried her and put a headstone over her that he learned her full name. Thomasina Plowright Coe. To him, to all

Donald Harington was born December 22, 1935, in Little Rock, took degrees at the University of Arkansas and Boston University, and did further graduate work at Harvard. He has taught in colleges in New York and Vermont and served as Distinguished Visiting Professor at the University of Missouri at Rolla. Currently, he is visiting professor at South Dakota State University. His novels include *The Cherry Pit* (1965), *Lightning Bug* (1970), *Some Other Place. The Right Place.* (1972), *The Architecture of the Arkansas Ozarks* (1975), and *Farther Along* (in press). He has published short stories in *Esquire* and included a selection of his own poems as a literary device in *Some Other Place. The Right Place.*, under the pseudonym Daniel Lyam Montross. Harington makes his home now in his automobile.

of them, she had just been Tommie. Until the summer it hurt her to walk, she walked the two miles into Stay More herself, once a month, and after stocking up on her month's staples at his grandmother's general store she would linger for an hour or more to chat with Gran and what other ladies might be there. He never listened to her; even if he were loafing around the store and could hear her plainly, her voice rising and falling with that particular lilt which was a gift of his people, he never *heard* her; he had no use for gabby old ladies. But then one day when he was loafing around the store, his grandmother said to him, "Vernon, if you're not doing anything else, could you take some things to Tommie? She isn't feeling too well." And his grandmother would take down from the shelves of her store sufficient for a month (although it never seemed so), and he would tote the gunny sack two miles up Swains Creek to Tommie's.

The first time, in June, she gave him a quarter and invited him to "set in the shade and visit a spell." He knew that if he declined and went on back to the store, his Gran would find some other work for him to do, so he sat in the shade of Tommie's maple tree and visited for a spell. Tommie gave him a couple of oatmeal cookies and all the cool well water he needed to wash them down. The yard was full of chickens who kept it bare of everything but dirt. She sat in a rocker which gouged parallel furrows in the earth. He sat on a maple stump stained with chicken droppings, but his old jeans were getting too small for him and he hoped to get rid of them somehow.

"Yessir," she started off, out of the blue, "he war the by-goddest feller ever they was."

"Who?" he asked.

"My man Tilbert," she replied. Young Vernon had not known she had been married; if she had, her husband must have been dead for all of Vernon's thirteen years. Now she was informing him voluntarily that he was "by-goddest," which can mean by-god wonderful or by-god terrible.

"How so?" he asked.

"Why, ever time he opened the door or shet the door, he would poot," she told him. He wondered if he had misheard her or if she were exaggerating.

"Poot?" he asked.

"Lord, yes! Tilbert could break wind anytime he wanted,

and he always did it ever time he opened the door or shet the door."

At thirteen Vernon had only finished the sixth grade and he knew that there were many phenomena of mankind past his ken. He was constantly questioning these, but he did not know if he wanted to know why a man would break wind each time he opened or closed a door. Still he asked:

"Why?"

"I'm a a-gittin to that," she said. "First I have to tell how come me and Tilbert got together to begin with."

And she proceeded to tell Vernon the entire story of her courtship and early marriage, which took her over an hour, and was halted only when he interrupted to say that Gran might be worrying that he had fallen in the creek and drowned or something and that he had better get on back to the store. The only interesting details of that hour-long story that he could remember were these: she was only fourteen when she married; Tilbert was fifteen years older than she, which made it seem all the more ludicrous that immediately after the wedding he began referring to her as his "old woman" and never called her anything else. She was still playing with dolls when she met him. She spent most of her spare time (what very little was left over from hard chores at the Plowright place) sewing fancy clothes for her small collection of tiny home-made dolls and one worn store-boughten doll. Vernon's impression was that this activity had not so much satisfied some maternal instinct in her as it had provided a vicarious escape from her own wardrobe, which had been spare and shoddy. When she first laid eyes on Tilbert Coe, he riding into the Plowright yard to inquire about buying a heifer, she was hemming the garment on one of her dolls. The first words Tilbert Coe said to her were, pointing at the doll, "I've got somethin you'd lak to play with a heap more'n thet thang," and a few days later, when she actually had played with it (although they would defer true intercourse until the bridal night), he asked her if that wasn't more fun than playing with dolls and she allowed that maybe it was but insisted on sewing clothes for it, which she commenced to do and continued to do for the rest of his life: fancy sacks, not dresses exactly, more like one-legged trousers in a suit, better clothing than the whole of he himself ever wore. Nobody ever knew about these "suits" except him and her . . . and, now, Vernon . . . although Vernon left her yard that day before ever finding out what it all had to do with Tilbert Coe breaking wind every time he opened or shut a door.

II

A month later, in July, one afternoon Gran said, "Vernon, I suppose it's about time you took some more things to Tommie," and he got the gunny sack and his grandmother checked off her list: ten-pound sack of flour, pail of lard, pail of sorghum, pound of sugar, cans of vienna sausages and sardines, and a spool of thread. He wondered how Tommie could live for a month on that meager larder, but he had noticed she had a small vegetable garden and of course there were the chickens all over the place, including the garden, where they ate most of the lettuce before it was mature.

It was a hot day, and he hadn't toted the sack more than a mile when he began to wonder if it was worth it, for just a quarter, and having to listen to Tommie talk about Tilbert. But when he got there she gave him fifty cents instead of a quarter, and to wash down the oatmeal cookies not just cool well water but cool sarsaparilla which she had made herself. They sat again in the shade of the maple tree and at once she resumed talking about her man Tilbert. He only half-listened, more preoccupied with trying to imagine what she had looked like at the age of fourteen when she was married. One by one Vernon fancied away her wrinkles, restored the darkness of her hair, returned the bloom to her lips and cheeks, and discovered that she was very pretty at the age of fourteen, just a year older than he. It made him suddenly uncomfortable, girl-shy as he was, so he transformed her back to her actual age. But to check the accuracy of his imagination, he interrupted her monologue to ask if she had a wedding picture of her and Tilbert. Just about every house in Stay More had one or more double portraits of old or dead couples when they were wed.

"No," Tommie said, "we'uns was jist too pore to hev our pitcher tuck." She didn't have a single picture of Tilbert, she lamented, although she had kept all of his "clothes," the fancy "suits" that she had sewn for his "doll," but she would be too "mortified" to show them to Vernon.

After their marriage, she said, Tilbert "bothered" her at least twice a day, right after the noon meal and again at bedtime, and on Sundays also on awakening and throughout the afternoon, and she suspected, although of course she never knew for sure, that he often "bothered" her while she was asleep at night. It was obvious that she didn't mind being "bothered," in fact enjoyed it enormously but was compelled to pretend otherwise, lest Tilbert suspect her of being "white-livered." Vernon hadn't heard that expression before, but two hours later, when he had succeeded in getting away from Tommie and back to the store, he waited until his grandmother had finished with a customer and then he asked her what it meant.

"White-livered?" Gran said. "Goodness, I haven't heard that for years. Where'd you hear it?"

"Tommie used it."

"Oh?" His grandmother looked pensive, but then she laughed. "Have you been listening to Tommie talk?"

"How can I avoid it, please tell me?"

Gran laughed again. "Poor Tommie. I guess she has no one to talk to these days but you, and that's only once a month. That's not too much, is it?" When Vernon allowed that he could stand it once a month, his grandmother told him what "white-livered" means. It was an old word that must have come from all the way back in ancient England. Nobody knew how you could tell if a woman's liver was white or not, but if it was, then it meant that the woman was so lascivious (Gran's word) that she would wear her husband to death. Did Vernon know what lascivious meant? Gran wanted to know. He said he could imagine.

Then he asked, "Did Tommie wear her husband to death?"

Gran's words jolted him: "Tommie was never married."

"But," he protested, "she claims she married Tilbert Coe."

"There've been plenty of Coes in the days of Stay More, but never one named Tilbert."

"Are you sure? That's what she said her husband's name was."

"Tommie never had a husband."

"Why not? She must have been very pretty when she was young."

"Oh, she was. She was very pretty. I can remember at least three fellows who wanted to marry her, and who courted her, but for some reason none of them ever married her."

"Maybe because she was white-livered?" he suggested.

"Now I wouldn't know about that," his grandmother said.

III

In August, for what was to be the last time, he toted the sack of groceries the two miles up Swains Creek to Tommie's. She was visibly frailer, and made no move to get out of her rocker but took the sack of groceries and set it down beside her rocker. She apologized, "I aint got any more oatmeal cookies fer ye. Aint been able to light a far in the stove."

"That's okay," he said, then offered, "Do you want me to light a fire for you?"

She shook her head. "Couldn't git to it, noway. 'Sides, it's hot, aint it? I'm cold as Christmas, but it's a right hot day, aint it?"

A mild breeze stirred the dust of her yard, but even in the shade of the maple it was hot. "Yes, ma'am," he said.

She reached inside her apron pocket and brought out a silver dollar, which she offered to him. He protested that that was too much for just a four-mile hike, but Tommie countered with:

"I caint take it with me."

"Where're you going?" he thoughtlessly asked.

She only stared at him for a moment and then said, "Lord knows."

They sat in silence for a while, looking at nothing, until he asked, "Is there any more to your story?"

She looked up and said, "Which story?"

"About you and Tilbert," he said.

"Oh, sure," she said, and it was soon obvious that she was not too frail to talk, and she picked up her "story" of Tilbert exactly where she had left off a month before, and continued it, through good times and bad, through drought and flood, seedtime and harvest, sunlight and moonlight, the stars, the mountains, the fields, the two-room house, the bed, where he finally died, in her arms, in the act of bothering her for the last time, at the age of seventy-two, leaving her a fifty-seven-year-old widow who would never be bothered again and would be lonesome for it.

Vernon asked, "Don't any of your children come to visit you or even write to you?"

She had not stopped talking as he spoke; their words were overlapped and she continued to the end of her sentence before stopping, then she said, "They are all dead too."

Vernon wanted to let her know that he knew she was just making up a story, but if a story was all her life had been, then he wanted even more to let her keep it. But he said, "You never did tell me why your husband pooted every time he opened or closed a door."

She smiled, as if remembering the thousands of openings and closings. Then she said, "I reckon it was jist his way of saying hello or goodbye." And she added, "I reckon it was jist proof that he was there."

"You didn't mind?" he wondered.

She smiled again. "It beat the daylights out of silence."

The late summer meadows and the roadside were full of the white diadems of the wildflower he knew as Queen Anne's lace, and before he left her he gathered a bouquet of Queen Anne's lace and presented it to her. "Why, thanks a heap," she said, clutching the bouquet to her chest, "that's right thoughty of ye." He knew she did not catch his thought of the symbolism of it: white flower, white liver, white lies.

Some time later, he put another large bouquet of Queen Anne's lace on her fresh grave, and no one commented upon the symbolism then, either. At least not to him. It was simply a pretty white and wild flower.

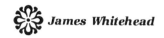 *James Whitehead*

The Travelling Picker's Prayer and Dream

Lord, forgive our drinking. Forgive our dreams
Of decency we can't shake off. Sisters
Are involved, and mothers, say our screams
That wake the whole bus up, and ministers
We come from haven't helped.

The poor are moral
But none of us have rotten teeth. Our teeth
Are good, washed by salt water. Fancy coral
Grows and forms what's called a barrier reef—
But what we're up against we can't be sure

Unless it is the sea, and the sea's too big
To drink to, and the sea's also impure
As Eve's mouth on the apple or Adam's fig.
Lord, a picker's dreams should not be cursed.
Remember the souls in the last hard town we blessed.

James Whitehead was born in St. Louis, Missouri, on March 15, 1936. He grew up in Mississippi and attended Vanderbilt University, where he took a B. A. in philosophy and an M. A. in English. After three years on the faculty of Millsaps College in Mississippi, and an M. F. A. in creative writing from the Iowa Writers Workshop, he joined the staff of the graduate writing program at the University of Arkansas in 1965. His first novel, *Joiner*, was published in 1971. His two volumes of poetry are *Domains* (1966) and *Local Men* (1979). Whitehead lives with his wife, Gen, and various of their seven children in Fayetteville, Arkansas, where he works on a sequel to *Joiner*.

Having Gained Some Spiritual Ruthlessness But Still Confused by What Has Happened A Local Man Considers a Friend Who Died Alone

He was a vain man and died courageously,
Except calling him vain defines the fault
As less than what it was. I've come to see,
Now he's in the ground, how he never meant

Much more than entertainment by the love
He gave us all. His death makes love a word
To be confused by. Mean, he had to prove
Our sympathy alone. His solitude

Toward the end was fancy cruelty—
His wife, his children and his friends shut out,
He would achieve the full catastrophe,
As sailors faced where Ocean Sea must quit.

Busy in the torn rigging of his heart,
He died, I hope, in a calm mortal sweat.

The Country Music Star Begins His Politics

There are no deadlier Americas
Than those I see from stages where I work,
And over coffee in the bad cafes,
Which is how everyone is going broke
Investing in good times and sentiment
Which pays my wages.
                              Squandering their love
The size of death and a revival tent
A troubled pride is what I have to give.

Whatever else they want they hardly say,
And I don't either. I am paid to strum
And make up songs that help grown children play.
The thing I do has prospered and gone wrong.
Lord, we are multiplied and we mean well.
There's murder in the darkness I can't kill.

Dealing with Mary Fletcher

1

Bolton Howard never served his time
Or anything. But he was strictly gifted
At dancing on a bill—
And thick as any pig he had three wives
Who if the word is right
Never saw him naked
And never wanted to.
He started with a ruined pulpwood truck
And once he wrecked his car and killed his child
By Mary Fletcher. He cried but didn't drink,
Which is insane,
Then sold his trailer park and went to hell.

2

After Mary Fletcher everything
Is pale, the story goes,
But no one gives details.
I used to watch her study clothes she bought
As if they might be fancy groceries.
She never tanned, for all the sun she took,
Who was as sensitive as gardening.
She married twice
And had good friends who always kept their tongues
Except to shudder when her name came up.
They never smiled.
I saw her buy three summer dresses once.

3

Hugo Lafayette Black
Once praised the legal mind of Albert Fletcher.
Judge Fletcher's opinions were written carefully
And his hedges were high as a goal
Because his troubled wife, a Methodist,
Was given to public tears for little reason—
And they never practiced anywhere but here,
And he raised his daughter almost by himself.
His wife before she died
Wrote a classic work on evidence

He took no credit for.
He wore a Panama and thick glasses.

4

I think all history
Revolves around my wife
Who says my head is like a ball of twine
I rarely use,
Or tape I lick until I gag. Her eyes
Are careless after life
But comforting in love,
And when I talk too much she won't put out.
Howard and the Fletchers piss her off.
I give her flowers twice a year, a brick
For Valentine's.
I give it in a sack.

5

Sometimes confusion in a private sorrow
Breaks a man. Davis is precisely that.
He was Mary's friend
But never came to much,
Considering the money he started with,
And Tulane Medical
And then a Jackson practice up until
Her child was killed. Connections are obscure.
He fell apart—
He lost his steady hand
Except for tying flies. He does that well
And writes pulp novels by another name.

 **Robert Dyer**

Poems on the I Ching

Chien: Obstruction

we have spent the day gathering wild herbs
waiting for the rain   for sunset   on the highest
ridge we pause   west is the sea   east
the fertile valley   north and south great cities
lie   the seed's shell splits   and still
there is no rain

Fu: Return

no wheel turns now   no Turner's Mill
and nearly now no concrete spillway
spring still flows cold though
spreads through water cress and jewel weed
to the iron wheel turning rusty   iron mandala
turns now   slowly turns

Hsiao Kuo: Preponderance of the Small

each briefest bird reminds me how i walk
beneath whatever thunder is   how slow
the body goes   the mind may leave to linger

Robert Dyer was born May 22, 1939, in Boonville, Missouri, on the
south bank of the Missouri River and has lived close to the river most
of his life. After twenty years at large, he has settled again in Boonville,
with his wife Rebecca (Moodie) Moon and their daughter Amber.
Oracle of the Turtle: Poems on the I Ching, from which this work is
selected, was published in 1977. He has produced a film (with
Michael Welber) entitled *Performing the Vision* and he writes songs.

with the rocks and animals   remember fire
the plants that heal   where water is   remember
what the turtle means

Pi: Grace

how easy here beside the creek
cold water spelling sun words
see how simply there it is
no matter what change makes it
and we think we don't know
anything

 *John Stoss*

Poem About a Farm Boy Who Went to College

And Returned to the Farm

Nothing is not enough but it circles every day
I try to hit it with clods when the plow chokes.
Supper's long over, dad and mom sleep, I sit
on the porch in overalls, crickets sing from
Chinese Elms that once deflected the sun,
now cover up the dark. Through a tree opening
all I can see of town are a few night eyes
moving around. In the daytime the town lies
crumpled like lovers' stripped-off clothing.

Tonight for an hour my mother talked about
all the bad daughters in that town and dad
said how telephone poles are rotting:
he sees them lean like vagrants
mouths cracked, hands outstretched or curled cold
making whip sounds that flail the night.
My Kafka lies beside the rocker, the sledge hammer
still beats behind the ears, I want to look
behind the canvas, not at the gramophone
where the tavern whines, but two thousand years ago
when the quick star spit coals which come to pass
on Disneyland in the dark—to turn the ferris wheel
that circles one way while I circle the other.
At the very top of the ride, a piece of paper
floats from my hand. North of here, coyotes read it.
Tomorrow is Sunday. When I get up at eight
the sun will already be pitched to the sky

John Stoss was born in Great Neck, Kansas, April 7, 1940. He
participated in the graduate writing program at the University of
Arkansas and for a number of years made his home in Fayetteville.
While he was there, he coordinated a local poets' and fiction writers'
reading series and directed a free university writers' workshop. His
first book of poems, *Finding the Broom*, was published in 1977 by Lost
Roads Press.

by a shovel as pigeons fly out of the bells:
we will be asked to pray for someone who dies.

Seven miles up the road lives John Pizer.
He tells stories: a lone mare who taunted
a bull into doing a stallion's work;
about two snakes coming toward each other
like armies, like ships, until the big
swallowed the small and two rabbits came along
and killed them both; about the wife
of old John who went to close the chicken
house and never came back: at night he sometimes
hears her creaking from the dark, cloudy
rafters of lice that are their own constellations.

My night ends the way the carnival ends:
the hot whine of motors and bells wind down,
the fat lady, who cannot dance, begins to snore,
the squeak and bounce of boats against the wall
in the tunnel of love is among the last late night
sounds of everything randomly coming to a halt:
the last dribble of milk from a cow's udder,
my piece of paper trapped among the thistles
in the ditch we burn every fall. Smoke
leans for miles pouring through
telephone wires into a blue sky.

What did my father say when I was born?
Why do pounding, migrating wings
circle above the night, and why does my life
startle and slip around me as I step
into a barn full of pigeons
shifting from rafter to rafter to rafter
among lice and snow white shit.

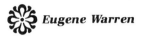 *Eugene Warren*

This Entangled Season

Stone petals unfold
in Spring twilight.
Tattered cloud-sheets restrain
the tumbling stars.
There are centuries between
the leaves of the crabgrass.
This entangled season
confuses: I walk across the street
to look back at my absence.
Birds fly through evening,
carrying in their beaks
coins struck
from the ashes of my heart.
The world in its silence
is too many for me,
despite the brief light shed
by image struck against fact.
The square of earth
lies within the circle of heaven,
man a pentangle inscribed inside—
a cyclist in the rain,
cubism of the soul.

Eugene Warren was born in 1941 in Craig, Colorado, and moved to Missouri in 1967 after graduating from Emporia State University. His books include *Christographia* (1973), *Rumors of Light* (1974), *Christographia 1–32* (1977), *Fishing at Easter*, and *Geometries of Light* (both in press). He has served as poetry editor of *Christianity and Literature* and editor of *GrafikTracts*. He lives in Rolla, Missouri, where he teaches at the Rolla campus of the University of Missouri.

 *Jack Butler*

Blackberries

I

The formal ocean has its watery hooks,
and here, in a sea of briars
far inland, certain repetitive themes occur,
water has pumped up plant and gotten its hooks in me again:
o primocane and floricane and dead old sticks, o thirst
for tantalant polyhedrals,
leaf-hidden, glimmering—packed purple beads
my eye can cull
from wrangle of shadow
somehow across a road! For here,
in the thrumming of a summer morning,
I'm makin' like a country boy, pickin' blackberries,
thinking of fatherhood and childhood
and lost time like energy gone form—
my father, I provide, provide (my fathers)
with a rolling of wrist, a trained mumble of palps
to fat clusters,
a dropping of plumpness to palm till palm brims,
must dump in bucket: enough moral
here for a preacher's boy

Jack Butler was born May 8, 1944, in Clarksdale, Mississippi, to Jack and Dorothy Niland Butler. In 1965, he moved to the foothills of the Missouri Ozarks, and in 1968, to Fayetteville, Arkansas, where he studied in the graduate writing program.

He has been an ordained Baptist preacher, fried-pie salesman, a carpenter, a graduate assistant English teacher, and is now data manager and science writer for the Cancer Cooperative Group of Northwest Arkansas and lives again in Fayetteville.

His poems have appeared in *Poetry, The New Yorker, Poetry Northwest, Southern Poetry Review, Texas Quarterly, Cavalier, New Orleans Review,* and many others. He has won second and first prizes in consecutive years in the *Black Warrior Review* fiction contest, and his poem, "Not Quite Like Son," was in *Best Poems of 1976.* A book of poems, *West of Hollywood,* was published in 1980 by August House Press.

with a child of his own twenty years later,
in how the one too many,
greedily plucked at, will tumble another
out of the hand, or how
the out-ventured hand, drawn suddenly back,
will make the barbs clamp, close inward together—
○ I am one to praise the very
thorns of the blackberry,
rose-cousin and edible tart fruit.
My mind drifts like a child's in visions of floating order,
my body attentive, sweat-beaded, mosquito-haunted—
these green canes, lashes,
sprung up limply on the wild rolled bramble,
the stiff persistent stuff
of its own past history—I hardly need
to say like a wave, processions of glimmering structure
there and not-there,
there at the corner of the eye,
to be gathered . . .

II

I ain't said nothin' about chiggers of course, horseflies
in relentless whizzing precession,
the possibility of moxicans or copperheads
somewhere under the interthreaded honeysuckle and
      greenbriar—
these forms that threaten invasion,
that are not merely there to be taken, lightly and
      imagistically taken,
but do their own taking.
Almost mathematically
one may mutter and permutate, by couple and couple: sumac,
blackberry brambles to bind it;
sumac and greenbriar; greenbriar and blackberry;
honeysuckle, its flowering spent, and sumac;
honeysuckle and sweetgum, whose stars,
immediate and thick as weeds, appear in the ditches;
greenbriar wound amid elderberry (now flowering)—
and what of triplets or the white dragonflies
with electric black wings
or blue slender naiads with dark blue glimmering wings,
the orders of lizards, rabbits,
or all of blue fulminant itchy summer
in one groined tree,
sumac groaning with bees, heavy-blossomed, in heat,

and me under it with ringing ears looking up
at branch-vaulted blue,
glad of the sweat-sodden weight of my denim,
at loose in the wild, uncomfortable, happy
to have made my escape, for once,
from breakfast?

III

Vine, bee, bramble, shrub, tree, and flower
in their tangled communion and trade create
a world, whose truth
is not a function exactly of pain or discomfort,
though I have come back
with hooks in my face, a sun-burnt nose, and later,
ankles nubbled with red-bug bites
a man will scratch bloody
to make quit itching: not a world whose harsh truth
poetry cannot enter,
but a world poetry must follow a man into—
let the barbs snag me, not my sent-out poem.
Let me have other than metaphorical blackberries,
let me shit seed,
bite down on a stink-bug
hidden in a handful of fruit.

IV

My daughter loiters at the pick-up,
the game gone dead for her
after the first few roadside fruit. What are we for,
growing older,
but to learn persistence in the right directions,
the useful stubbornness
no child can manage,
the pains to take
for the sake of a deep, original game?
I think now of my father's sermons
in all those backwoods churches, hard seats and
    dragged-out hymns,
two-week revivals he had to get it up for
after a hundred two-week revivals,
worrying about making a living and knowing himself
a sinner as bad as any he scolded,
his children wrong.
And I was the fat, unpleasant oldest, lazy, book-ridden,
swearing by dreams, wrong-headed,

itching with sleazy and sexual ignorance.
The hard-core faithful to prayer-meeting came
on Wednesday nights,
the richest of nights, the church close-grained with pews,
spilling a yellow radiance to sparse grass
as the deacons smoked and talked
and crops and spiders and kingdoms rose in the talk
and crumbled away, and, as I wrote
in a fralme t that has long since crumbled,
mosquitoes rose
like angels in the darkening woods, and sang.
Those roads, my daughter, we lived down,
those gravel trails with a church
or store with gas-pumps
or little town
at a humming focus, the backway,
haunted with wooden bridges and tree-shadow,
were Jerusalem's conduits then—
I thought we brewed the world's change
and new meaning.
I didn't know. It was been hard
to lose those meanings
and keep my own, but the rest of the world
does exist: I am not much
of a country boy, except—
under cool leaves.
Bend over, twist your neck, look up.
I am sorry about the mosquitoes, my daughter,
the dust, the blazing sun, the hard sharp rocks,
the stink of dead animals.
Your father's a poet and not a preacher.
Not much difference—we roll our own.
Like cobwebs
a man walking through trees
breaks with his face, those little roads
are broken and gone
on the face of the round world's present. But what poetry
has had for me
more beauty or order or mystery
than that we thought of in wooden churches
late at night
under the stars, our odd harmonic cries
troubling the owls?

V

The other night,
out at the place,
the new place,
the one we will own in two years,
our first,
alone, preparing to sleep
in the moon-barred cabin (its logs unchinked),
exhausted and solitary,
spooky,
putting in time
to make it our home
the chuck-will's-widow
whipping its call,
the cat snoring,
I thought of my crimes: I imagined monsters
loose in the woods,
thought of the methodist graveyard
across the road,
the bodies gathered and packed and crumbling,
and thought, somehow,
of that whole cemetery,
chambered with death—
from which I imagined
skeletons rising,
cackling with their own lost crimes,
to come at my scalp
through the moonlit door—
as a fruit like a blackberry, rich with form,
composite. And slept.

Apology for Hope

I

Mostly the imposition of geometries,
this building Home. With a shovel I imagine
a shoveled rectangle for under-floor—
bite by bite, the spade reveling
in divot on green-capped black divot
laid shingle-wise on the topsoil mound—
why waste what beans can use?

II

And I have caused to rise joists
in the jessamine air—repeats of rectangle,
simplest relation for a novice: grey rough-cuts
from a split barn, shaggy with age,
resume in one harmonium (sort of)
with the clean slender wands of soft pine
they sell for two-by's downtown.

III

Holes and tunnels in the salvage lumber—
all homes crawl with Home,
bumblebee and termite chew holes in Euclid,
even thought's bones host thought: the axes,
axed open, brew with disorder, virus.
Where's hope if what takes us has none?

IV

Throttled in rose-thorn and bayberry, the bootlegger's
crumbling chimney, ablaze with bees.
I won't use it or tear it down. *You almost,*
John said, seeing how near I built,
have a fireplace.
                    A house
burned here once, that sudden bloom
drowned under forty springs of change.
Their pond I go down to to drink, ripe now
with algae, bullfrogs, small bream spanking

green runs open in pollen,
emerald holes in silks of rainbow. The government,
in the thirties, paid them to build it.

I spade up soot-black, melted jars.

V

Here is a hill where buzzards sail close
in soft blue over froth of plum-bloom.
In its flank I frame slowly our great hope,
the oldest, most banal, deepest, most sweet.
It is what those rust-skinned roots were dreaming of
when my shovel, heel-driven, made moons of severance
across them, and I tore them like dirty rope
out of the black, odorous ground.

 *Jim Bogan*

Missouri Litany

Belle, Bland, Boss & Doss
Competition, Concord, Leeper & Sleeper
Now ain't it Peculiar
from Aaron to Zwanzig
run the names of Missouri

Apex, Palace & Harmony
Slabtown, Skintown & Economy
Tightwad, Turtle & Tuxedo
from lordly Duke to lowly Elmo
run the names of Missouri

Forget the passport here's where you go:
    Brazil, California, Eden & El Dorado
    Havana, Atlantis, Dublin & Dixie
    Nevada, Westphalia, Congo & Syracuse
    Punjaub, Damascus, Cairo & Cabool

Halfway between Bolivar
(rimes with "Oliver")
and Buffalo

Jim Bogan writes of himself: "Born at dawn on September 9, 1945, by the shores of Lake Michigan and grew up in a willow tree. Learned how to play third base, instead of the violin. Educated in Catholic schools, Chicagoland, Rome, Kansas, and the Ozarks. Ph.D. from the University of Kansas after years of studying William Blake, a fire source. Dissertation: 'A Guidebook to Blake's Jerusalem,' maps included. Teaches writing, film, books, and art at the University of Missouri-Rolla for a living. Loves boats without motors, music with saxophones, hard work, and no work at all. Surprised into being a writer at age twenty-eight. One book so far: *Trees in the Same Forest*, cedars included, and another on the way: *Ozark Meandering*. Keeps a clear desk, but near to hand and eye are: pictures of children and angels; a star chart; three dictionaries; a cream pitcher full of pens and screwdrivers; chert arrowheads; a two-foot cedar in a coffee can, sun-and-moon painted by daughters and sons; and out the window: oaks, a creek, hills and the Ozark sky floating by."

is Halfway and
down the road is Fairplay
and around the bend is Bona,
that's "Bonny"

Some nervous citizens reformed Sodom to Dildy Mill
Land-Office propaganda twisted Snake County to McDonalds
Look Out, Aromatic Creek is a cover for Ol'Stinky
Whoop-Up got busted to Sapp
while Tick Crick tenaciously remains Tick Crick

Versailles, just like it looks
yet Pomme de Terre is merely a potato in Paris,
France, that is.
The Chamber of Commerce of Commerce
Rolyat, that's Taylor spelled backwards
Libertarians burn books in Liberty
while the Devil's Racetrack is in . . .
the heart of Christian County

    Acid & Cyclone
    Clever & Covert
    Gunboat & Rosebud
   Devil's Elbow & Angel's Wing
   Regal, Rat, Chloride & Cannan
   Slapout, Smackout, Dent & Damsel
   run the names of Missouri

 **Paul Johnson**

let her travel far

let her travel far
let some witch show her
in every forest burns
a burning bush
hedge-apple hexagrams
stars like dragons
streams like time
the mosses' greens
tree in a cliff
hawk's quick lift
bones beneath sky
stare of owl's eye
summer is best
live's in the chest
spirits in fogs
of a rotting log
nothing remains
except the grain
let her travel far
let some witch show her

Paul Johnson was born September 12, 1945, in Galesburg, Illinois, where he spent his school days. He took degrees at Knox College and the University of Kansas, and since 1970 has lived in Rolla, Missouri, where he teaches at the Rolla campus of the University of Missouri. His poems have appeared in a number of literary journals.

 **Leon Stokesbury**

To All Those Considering Coming

To Fayetteville

Often these days, when my mind holds splinters
like the pieces of the shampoo bottle
I dropped and shattered yesterday, I think
of other places. It is wintertime now,
and the Ozarks are hushed up with snow
everywhere. They are small mountains, almost
not mountains at all, but rather, with trees
sticking up, they seem more like
the white hairy bellies of fat old men
who have lain down here. What has this to do
with anything? I don't know. Except
it makes me think of snow elsewhere, and what
it would be like to be there. I might drive
across Oklahoma, then on into
New Mexico. I could be there tonight.
The land would be flat, the snow over
everything. The highway straight, and forever
the snow like blue cheese in the moonlight,
for as far as there is, and air, cold air
crisp as lettuce, wet lettuce in the store,
and I would keep driving, on and on.

Leon Stokesbury was born in Oklahoma City on December 5, 1945. He was raised in southeast Texas, but spent most of a decade in Fayetteville, Arkansas, where he took his M. A. in English and M. F. A. in creative writing from the University of Arkansas. In 1975 he was one of the three winners of the first Associated Writing Programs Annual Poetry Competition; his manuscript, *Often in Different Landscapes*, was published the next year by the University of Texas Press. In 1979 he published a chapbook, *The Drifting Away of All We Once Held Essential*, with Trilobite Press in Denton, Texas, while he was poet-in-residence at North Texas State University.

In 1980 he joined the faculty of Hollins College in Virginia. He especially notes that he enjoys preparing and eating French food.

Sometimes

Sometimes in summer, I lie in bed, just
at dawn, and just outside my window I
see the morning strike the trees' leaves
in a way that lets me blur my sight, until
I see, not trees, but canyons of yellow
and green; or, if not canyons, water then,
maybe water falling, with the sun's glint
glancing off, as it does off spray, or it
could be white lava, or green. Then the day.

 *Speer Morgan*

The Bad Cat

Late in the afternoon of her seventy-first birthday Dr. LaVerne Sparks looked out her kitchen window and, seeing movement behind the snow-covered woodpile in her backyard, put down a marker that she had been using to label tin cans full of oddments and went to the utility closet. There she unwrapped the Winchester carbine her father had taught her to shoot in 1914. From an oily box kept since her father's death, she extracted three shiny bullets and loaded the rifle, not at the moment remembering that they were new, purchased six weeks before and transferred into the box, but feeling them as his bullets—the single carton he had left when he died. She felt his presence strongly as she cocked the gun, remembering the smell of dirt, tobacco, and sweat on him as he stood beside her and with grinding impatience demonstrated how to load and shoot the rifle. When she finally hit the tin can she did not understand why he knelt, took painful hold of her shoulder and said, "We will have to provide." And she did not yet understand that the wildness in his face had come from the

---

Speer Morgan writes: "I was born in Fort Smith, Arkansas, in 1946. My mother was of local establishment stock and my father a Yankee. I went to the University of the South for two years, where my roommate introduced me to his grandfather Allan Tate, whose mysterious fragility convinced me that I should be a writer rather than a lawyer.

I then went on to the University of Arkansas, and to Stanford. In 1970 I became a staff book reviewer for *Rolling Stone* and continued that task until 1973. For the past several years I have co-directed the creative writing program at the University of Missouri and am presently serving as editor of the *Missouri Review*.

In 1976, I published a volume of short stories, *Frog Gig and Other Stories*, and in 1979, *Belle Starr: A Novel* met with some success domestically and with overseas publishers (England, Argentina, Italy). In 1979, I won the *Prairie Schooner* award for the best story in their magazine that year ("Internal Combustion"). My second novel, tentatively titled *Small Money*, will be published by Atlantic, Little Brown in fall, 1981."

doctor who had just visited and had given Solomon Sparks the first and last physical examination of his life. She thought only of escaping his grasp and the expression in his face, not her father's but some crazy man's, some Methodist's at an outdoor meeting staring dizzy rings at her, saying, "You will not forget. You will not. There are no sons," then walking away from her and standing at the edge of the newly plowed field as if he had suddenly forgotten what he was doing.

She did not remember that they were new bullets, which had cost her more than a week of embarrassment, carrying the old rifle in a cloth wrapper around the city—so changed since her retirement from the university that several times she got lost and was forced to ask gas-station attendants to call cabs for her. Once she forgot her address and entirely lost her composure. If her younger sister discovered that LaVerne was wandering the streets carrying an old rifle, she would take her without further ado to St. Louis. She was just waiting for an excuse. And so before her final expedition for bullets, in case she should again forget herself, LaVerne taped a label to her wrist that said Call Cab, 911 Bright Street. Clerks were suspicious when she unwrapped the rifle and asked for shells to fit it. They referred her to worried-looking managers who denied having such shells and recommended other stores, the names of which she printed in the bold rectilinear script she had struck across blackboards for forty-five years in the school of agriculture. She was proud of the script. It still came easily.

Although at times her memory was vivid and insistent, spreading beyond a corner of her mind into her eyes and fingertips, it was no longer reliable. At good moments she knew this, and so with the script cared for herself, labeling household items, and arranging them carefully, even things she knew should not have to be labeled, like the clock—a strip of tape pointing to 6 saying Sunday Bess Calls, a reminder to prepare for the weekly examination that her younger sister gave her by telephone from St. Louis. And with the script she noted the names of hardware and sports stores recommended by the uneasy clerks and managers, hoping they noticed, saw it as an instrument of clarity.

She finally obtained bullets from a man who did reloading for gun hobbyists, having prepared beforehand and neatly delivered to him the third lie of her life—excepting those she had told before her father's death and now told her sister every week to escape being sent to St. Louis. She had first lied regarding her age, in 1918, to a bemused dean of agriculture at the University of Missouri. He was disturbed partly by her youthful appearance and partly by the fact that she had walked the gravel turnpike twenty miles from Rocheport alone, but even more because she was a woman and he, against all regulation and sentiment, for no good reason either political or personal, was admitting her to the school of agriculture. The second lie was a continuation of the first: the age she noted on a teaching contract offered by the same dean four years later. And this, the third, was spoken simply, a few words that she had memorized for the man with bullets: "It is for my husband. He is a gun hobbyist."

*   *   *

Gripped by the memory of her father's potato-rough hand, her fingers trembled as the lever clicked shut, and she crept back to the window. Jewel purred loudly, nervously pacing the kitchen, and stroking against LaVerne's ankle. There was no movement visible now, although she seemed to discern tracks in the new snow leading from behind the woodpile to the house. The setting sun cast a deep orange light across the snow. "Fire before night," she whispered to herself.

She shifted her attention to the basement, where he had been coming into the house by night and recently by day. At night he waited until she had turned off her bedroom light and gone to bed. Usually he awakened her from the first drowse of sleep—the time, like waking, when her mind plunged through a miracle of crazy pictures—awakened her by the clinking of a spoon on Jewel's plate. Then he would move quietly across the hardwood floor, less in steps than the lifting of steps, sometimes into the hall and toward her room, through the doorway and to the foot of her bed. If already asleep, she felt his presence as a dream or a thing surrounding her dreams. At other times she was fully awake, hearing the slightly asthmatic rattle of his breath and imagining the slow blink of his yellow eyes. She would lie rigid in his presence rather than get up, for she had vowed not to do anything sudden or out of the ordinary that might result in a broken hip or leg. More than once she had lain without moving while he attacked Jewel.

It was the stench in the house that had finally driven her out for bullets—not for poison because Jewel might be the victim rather than the black tomcat, nor help from students who lived in the neighborhood because among them were foreigners and strange young men with beards—not these, but bullets for the rifle she had learned to shoot sixty years ago and never yet had reason to use. The stink was from the black tomcat. She scrubbed the floors with chemical disinfectant and shut Jewel's basement window, galled by this necessity since it was her custom to allow the animal free access outside. She had never doted on Jewel; they retained a distance that seemed mutually acceptable, the cat assuming the role of pet only at feeding times, when begging was necessary to remind the woman of her existence and need. The woman liked the animal as a farmer may like a worthless dog, less to fondle or prattle at or even watch than merely to coexist with, taking some enjoyment in the presence of other warm blood.

It irritated LaVerne when the cat rubbed against her leg. "Stop," she whispered, now listening at the basement door. It was irritating, too, to think of the basement, where several weeks ago the black tomcat had broken Jewel's shut window—as she imagined, hurling himself yellow eyes and face first through the solid pane of glass so that he could continue to bother her, an act confirming his strangeness, perhaps aberrance. Hearing the window break, she had taken the rifle and new bullets to the basement, there sat down in a lawn chair, which she had bought upon retiring and never used, and waited for the cat to show his face. The window had been broken from inside, indicating the tomcat had been locked in the basement when she shut Jewel's window three days before—locked *in*, not out. Waiting with the rifle, she imagined the cat pacing in darkness three days, ferreting for sustenance that did not exist in her clean basement, finally pushing, scratching on the place of light; then she saw—imagined— him back up, gather himself, and ram his whole weight against the glass, shattering it. No cat should do this.

Later she searched among shelves of labeled equipment for caulking compound and glass to fix the window. She found glass and a cutter but was unable to find the compound, and her determination to patch the window flagged as she began to lose herself among labels. Discovering boxes and cans of equipment that needed rearranging, she took them out and sat amidst the clutter with her tape and marker, intending to reshuffle it, once again to know exactly what was in her house. There were labels that puzzled her, boxes of things she did not remember putting away. On a shiny tin can the script—hers, unmistakably—read: Decorations, 4/10/68; inside were pinecones, nothing else, and she dumped them into the trash. A larger can, empty, was labeled Cherry Pie, 1/25/70. She ripped off the tape. The entire method of arrangement seemed strange, in fact impractical, and so she began anew the task of ordering things, moving from closet to closet and shelf to shelf, unpiling and emptying boxes and cans in the floor.

With cabinet nails that had been in storage since March 1942 and planks separately labeled 1 inch x 6 inches x 4 feet, she built new shelves in the utility closet. In the basement she pulled a standing shelf away from the wall so that it could be reached from both sides. She made lists and pored over them trying to establish the best plan, sitting at her old desk with sketches and outlines; the ink on her nib pen repeatedly drying as she tried to envision a perfect order—the more stubborn her determination, the more impossible the task. It was too much finally, not in physical quantity but in the meticulousness of her demands, and after several days of losing herself in traps of minuteness, falling into black holes between holes between things that had floated into nonsense, fearing that the cat would return and walk among her exposed things, sniff them, step on them or even worse, she abandoned her project and put things away as best she could.

There was no sound in the basement. She leaned the rifle in the corner, went out the back door and down the steps into the snow. Less concerned about small illnesses like colds and flu than certain larger things—accidents—LaVerne often, as now, neglected to put on her coat. At the woodpile she picked out three good logs, knocked the snow off, and carried them inside. She carried the weight easily. Back outside, she chopped kindling with a well-sharpened hatchet, her vigorous blows echoing into the silence of new snow. It was a blessing when snow made the student-infested neighborhood clean and quiet. Stopping and listening, she observed tracks around the house and followed them to the broken basement window. On all windows but this one she had placed storm fittings. She had leaned the last fitting against the wall and left the broken window open. Now she knew why. Carefully she bent over, gazing into the dark basement, and put the storm fitting into place. If he was in there now, he was trapped.

Back inside, she listened at the basement door, then shut it. After laying and setting a fire, she placed the screen in front of it and went into the bathroom. It was her birthday, and Sunday, and her sister would be calling around 6 P.M. She turned on the tub water and began taking off her clothes. A bath each Sunday relaxed and prepared her for the examination. Not that she was nervous—she was never so much that as steadily tense, vigilant—a quality that in recent years had forsaken her, or turned bad, as boundaries and delineations and even words themselves sometimes evaporated, and the vigilance lost center, turned in circles, becoming a blank dizzy tightness that wanted somehow to shatter. She always felt that way when her sister called and so took the soothing bath beforehand. In order to pass she had to keep her senses about her, answer the questions properly, and perhaps inquire about the grown nephews whose names she had taped onto the wall. It was just a friendly call. But she knew the stakes; her sister had made that clear.

She hung out a fresh towel and saw that the shade was securely drawn. She could not be too careful of her privacy, for strangely dressed young people walked across her property at all hours, presumably university students but often of such slovenly appearance, poor posture, and ragged clothing, that they seemed less students than poor farm children, offspring of sixty acres and antiquated techniques, of farms that refused or were unable to afford the benefits of science, like her own father's—children like those with whom she had gone to school in Rocheport before and during the Great War, who came to school streaked with mud and stinking of animals, went to sleep in class because they had been up doing chores since before sunrise, whose teeth turned green and sometimes broke off into their food. As a teacher she had fought rural mismanagement for forty-five years, and it disturbed her to see college students in the guise of poverty, all the worse since it was false. Dirty, unkempt young people loping across her yard were like ghosts out of that old time—false ghosts mocking the resolution and task of her life.

She ran hot water until the temperature was suitable, then carefully stepped into the tub. Warmth settled into her hips and legs as she lay back against the curve. Through the open door the living-room fire crackled. Jewel appeared, eyes wide, tail high, and began rubbing back and forth against the door frame. "Away!" She flicked water at the cat and it scampered out. She liked privacy in the bath. Hooking a green rubber hose onto the tap, she adjusted a moderate flow to keep the water warm, a gentle ruffle of pressure against her where the hose happened to rest.

The first noise in the basement did not register with LaVerne. She had already become unmoored, as she often did in the bath, without pause or transition breaking into pure reverie, a state no longer willed nor purely enjoyable but habitual, as if entering the tub turned some switch in her mind. It delighted and scared her, like the dreams she had had as a child before her father's death. She often thought of him—the image of him, as now, skating beside her down Penson's Creek at night, one month and two days before he was to get up from breakfast coughing, go outside to the woodpile, lean against it, and hemorrhage through the mouth—skating with the ease that he had learned as a young man in Chicago, a clerk who dreamed of mansions and empires and of courting rich young ladies, before he dropped it all and came back to a small farm in a dying town in mid-Missouri to live out his life—skating with his hands clasped behind, swaying rhythmically even as he rounded curves in the crooked frozen creek, his moon shadow a vague blur across the ice. He had bought the ice skates in Columbia, a full day's journey to and fro by wagon. Hers were two sizes small, but she did not complain. She jammed them onto her feet, amazed that he had gone off and bought them, had stomped in the front door at suppertime and handed them to her, demanding that she put them on. He paced the living room and coughed while she tied the laces. In twenty minutes they were out on Penson's Creek; her knock-kneed and stumbly, afraid that someone might see her; him worriedly explaining and demonstrating the basics of skating. She picked it up quickly, carried by the force of his will to have her suddenly *know* how to skate, whisking up behind and holding her, virtually lifting her from the ice and moving with her until her ankles were solid. Past the edge of town the creek widened and flowed through bottomland toward the Missouri River. Her father pointed at a slash of moon on the ice ahead of them and said, "Catch it!" Hurrying to keep up with him, she forgot to be awkward, leaned with him into the numb air, chasing the running white moon's reflection, no sound in the widening creek but the keening of their skates and his harsh breath. She strained to catch the moon, but then only to keep up with him, as the creek broadened and neared the river. It cracked around them and he headed her off. "Can't go no farther," he said. "We're too close now." They stood for a moment listening to the flow of the ice-choked river. Her father began to cough, and they headed back.

This time the noise was too loud not to register. She sat up very straight in the tub, the dream on her face becoming puzzlement. The sound repeated, echoed, as if to bring her back to now. Something very bad was happening, something breaking. She looked at the white enclosure around her, the fluid. Heat pressed uncomfortably against the inside of her thigh, where the green thing lay. Still confused, she reached out and turned knobs. Heat bloomed out of the green hose. Dark holes began to flare around her. She was standing. A thing ran across the floor in the other room.

She was dressed in something. She had a thought: I am dying. She held onto that thought but did not believe it. Now was the trial. She stood in the living-room doorway, looking at a thing above the fire. She looked at it until she understood what it was. It was her pet on the mantelpiece. "Jewel," she said. The couch spoke softness to her. Her legs were weak. But now was the trial that she had faced before, how many times she did not know, as around her little holes of darkness continued to burst. She stood in front of the wall clock in an effort to remember something, but its ticking seemed to slow down, its hands to slip. She acted.

The thing in her hands became a gun, and she leveled it, spitting a bullet onto the kitchen floor. She remembered that more were in it. Dizziness receding, she opened the basement door, turned on the lights, and started down the steps.

The animal was around her, claws against concrete, now flying through the shelf, arching, exploding in tin cans and jars out the other side, running against the wall and gone, hidden in a dark place. A can rolled in a circle and was still. Glancing through the litter, she felt herself slipping. *"You are a bad cat,"* she said out loud, startled by her own words. Approaching the other side of the basement, she held the gun ready to shoot. He was hiding under the other half of the house, where the basement ended and dirt lay within two feet of the floor joists. Her foot stung, evidently cut by a piece of broken glass, but she did not raise it for fear of losing her balance. She had not known that she was barefoot. The basement was a clutter. As the sting reached upward, her body became real, clarified, and the rifle settled into her hands, no longer an abstraction wielded like a stick in a dream but a rifle. It was cold. She realized that she was wet. At the concrete wall where the basement ended, she saw the cat. A moment before in frenzied movement, he now sat hunched in the dirt directly facing her about fifteen feet away, blinking his eyes lazily, apparently without fear. She could hear the slight rattle of his breath. She aimed at his face.

At that moment two things happened. The phone began to ring upstairs and she realized something: if the cat were shot under the floorboards she would not be able to get him out. It would be dangerous for her to clamber over the wall and through the dirt after him. But the phone was ringing quite insistently. She continued to aim at the cat's face. He seemed unconcerned. His yellow eyes blinked again, as if he were about to take a nap. It occurred to her that if she did not shoot him now she never would.

It was not in her nature to be indecisive, and so each moment longer—the ringing all in her ears—her irritation mounted toward decision. Now the cat did something strange. He got up and turned his back to her, then hunched down again. He looked up at the window that he had broken weeks before, now sealed by the storm fitting. It was dark outside. He was a big cat, well muscled but with a dull, ragged coat. She was aiming now at his back and the base of his upturned head. He seemed to be waiting for the window to open. Intervals between each ring of the phone got longer.

"You are a bad cat," she scolded, with one eye shut and the wooden stock against her cheek. She pulled the trigger not as her father had taught her but in a jerk, and the gun burst across the hollow space, in a single instant picking the cat up by the spine and snapping him in a perfect somersault. The shock of the explosion died into the ringing phone, and she tried to turn from the cat and go upstairs. On his back he wallowed spasmodically in the dirt, like a giant bug trying to flip himself over.

She turned and walked carefully through the litter toward

the staircase. She would not run to catch the phone but would be careful, would hold the railing, and take each step at a time. And now at the bottom of the stairs, she would not falter at the sound—the dull thud that she heard behind her. But neither could she take the first step. There was no further sound— only the ringing phone upstairs—but she knew something was wrong. A terrible, sweet weakness loosened in her chest and spread. She smelled her father's breath, suffused with the odor of the black liquid that he carried in a bottle in his pocket during the last months and sometimes drank to giddiness. She was astonished by him when he got that way, when he laughed at dinner, coughed and laughed, mumbling that he was dying and then laughing more—a grotesque joke that made her and the younger sisters laugh, too, they who were old enough by then—or who lived in a time when at their age they could know—that he was not merely joking. And him tickling her with his rough, snub hands, the only part of him that was the same, the rest an impersonation by someone younger than her father who grinned strangely and seemed, at the last, a little silly.

Now she heard a quick shallow rattle of breathing behind her. She turned and was not surprised to see the cat walking across the basement floor toward her. He came sideways, his rear feet advancing independently of his forefeet. His head down like a mule in harness, he approached her. LaVerne tried to cock the rifle. But then the cat's rear feet walked faster, and he turned in a circle and sat down among shards of glass. His back and part of his head were exploded, ridiculously un-zipped. He fell onto his side and shuddered, was for a moment still, then reached out with one paw, stretching his claws and slowly pulling inward as if to bring something to himself.

The phone had stopped ringing. LaVerne walked carefully, right foot and right foot, up the stairs. In the kitchen she put the rifle into its cloth. On the couch in the living room she sat down. Jewel stared brightly at her from the mantelpiece. She waited for the fire to warm her. The phone would ring soon, and she began to prepare for her sister, the tiny irritating voice that would jabber from the receiver. She thought of what she would say. The cat continued to stare at her, making her uncomfortable. She looked at the cut on her foot. It needed care. Her glance fidgeted around the room and then up again at the wide-eyed cat.

 **_Karlene Gentile_**

Leaf and Stone and Wind

I.

I want to feel the magic
of this October Sunday in Missouri
here in this landscape
of limestone, moss and maple,
learn the silence of a creek
expecting rain, the silence
of trees rooted, fixed,
enduring the arrogance of hawks.
I need humility. I need the spirit power.
But my fists are knots.

II.

Who can know, along this tangled bank,
this ironwood and persimmon, who can know
while I kneel at a table
next to you, arranging wildflowers
in a vase, who in the opulent aura
of evening could know, while you dust
my skin with pollen, you lean into winter
angular and cold.
                    Your gun blasts me out of sleep.
The telephone rings an eternal nightmare of disaster.
There is no magic anywhere.

III.

In town I walk the evenings on the women's college
grounds across the street. From the lighted rooms
I hear music, laughter, voices. A girl practices

Karlene Gentile was born in Chicago November 11, 1946. In 1964
she moved to Boone County, Missouri, took her master's degree in
literature at the University of Missouri and made the state her home.
She is editor of Singing Wind Press/K. M. Gentile Publishing and
teaches at the University of Missouri in St. Louis.

her flute. Her notes are like rain washing the dust
off leaves. The voices of girls in their rooms
float and circle me, linger on the leaves,
the mums, curl along benches where lovers
plan the future. They land on leaves, words
looking for a sentence.

You sent your voice around the wings of a heron
waiting at the edge of water. You left feathers
I could gather.
                    All this flash of fall is illusion.
It is a barren season.

IV.

A friend brings me tomatoes. The are small
and green. 'They will ripen in the window. They
will be sweet and good' he says. Later, driving
in the country, he tells me about the Sioux.
They wandered to mourn death. They left the tribe
giving away everything until they had nothing left
but their sorrow. When they returned, they
brought back the power of the Spirit. Gifts
were given them and there was a celebration.

The day is alive with color. Ready cornfields,
endless gold. There will be frost soon. There is
wood to cut and fires to burn in the stoves
of friendly houses.
                    Outside, as the universe turns
brute white, you move through the dark place,
elemental, leaf and stone and wind.

 **Jon Looney**

The New Savage

A pale face
paddling downriver
will be red
as sunset tonight.

The rest
of vacation:
redfaced
under shade trees,
observing the initiation
of other braves.

There is,
sitting on a shaded
rock, time
to think.

In the rushing water
and in bird-calls,
New Savage
hears the tom-tom
of a former tribe.

A pulse
in his head
attempts to take up
the rhythm.

Jon Looney was born on the first of March, 1948, in Trumann, Arkansas and attended The School of the Ozarks in Missouri and Arkansas State University. His books of poems include *Uphill* (Arrow Press, 1971), *Headwaters* (1979), and *Bluffwalker, Snakedoctor, Whistlepig* (1980), the last two from August House. He lives in Batesville, Arkansas.

 **Walter Bargen**

Meta, Mo.

With its charcoal factory in ashes
barbershop open alternate days
The General Merchandise and Fancy Groceries
moved into memory
Main Street is at the end of town.

In front of the bank
two cars are a parade
one smile a good day.

Through the curtainless cafe window
its one pinball machine
is busy all day
ringing tilted on a sagging floor.

Walter Bargen was born July 20, 1948. He writes: "I have lived in Missouri for the last twenty years and over half of that in Boone County (geologically the northernmost edge of the Ozarks); before that in North Carolina and Germany. I graduated from the University of Missouri (1970) with a degree in philosophy and spent a year in graduate school (anthropology) at Rutgers from which I was drafted and served two years as a conscientious objector. After that it was a series of short jobs: library clerk, bicycle mechanic, and finally carpenter, which I continue to do for a living. (I started with my own house.) I have two children, Cedar, my son, and Kale, my baby daughter. I became seriously involved with writing poetry around 1972." A volume of Bargen's poems, *Fields of Thenar*, was published in 1980.

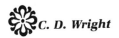 **C. D. Wright**

Obedience of the Corpse

The midwife puts a rag in the dead woman's hand,
takes the hairpins out.

She smells apples,
wonders where she keeps them in the house.
Nothing is under the sink
but a broken sack of potatoes
growing eyes in the dark.

She hopes the mother's milk is good a while longer,
and the woman up the road is still nursing.
But she remembers the neighbor
and the dead woman never got along.

A limb breaks,
She knows it's not the wind.
Somebody needs to set out some poison.

She looks to see if the woman wrote down any names,
finds a white shirt to wrap the baby in.
It's beautiful she thinks
like snow nobody has walked on.

C. D. Wright was born in Mountain Home, Arkansas, January 6, 1949, and lived in the Ozarks except for brief periods until 1979, when she moved to northern California. After she graduated from the writing program at the University of Arkansas, she stayed on in Fayetteville and became associated with Lost Roads Press, which in 1977 had published her second volume of poems, *Room Rented by a Single Woman*, as its initial volume. Her other books are *Alla Breve Loving*, from Mill Mountain Press in 1976, and *Terrorism*, a 1979 volume from Lost Roads. She assumed the management of Lost Roads after the death of Frank Stanford.

Room Rented by a Single Woman in

Van Buren, Arkansas

She set her nightcream on father's short wave
Soon as she said her name I knowed
She was Mennonite
I said Your Brothers and Sisters left here
The whole flock took off
Last year vegetables was sold on the square
Headed for somewhere runover with bandits and fever
She said She didn't have brothers
Her twin was a stillborn
Furthermore
She wouldn't be caught dead wearing black
Unless it was a slip
Or a strapless
I said I didn't allow no smoke
She said She took rose hips for breakfast
I looked at her curls pouring over her combs
I could see the husbands leaving the barbershop
Walking to their office
They'd be saying her name
When they looked for their seals
They'd be phoning their bookie
They'd be betting their pots on her honey
I bit my tongue I was going to ask
Why she come back she said She knew this town
She knew where Ramsey shelved the strychnine
How he cut the corduroy short
Where the sweetgum roots broke the sidewalk up
How Doctor Bruno backs his buick down Second Street
Where the Jew was buried and how his grave washes out
I moved in on her close I knowed
She couldn't see
I passed my emery board in front of her face
She couldn't see shit
I could feel her breasts
Giving in like snow under a boot

 *Frank Stanford*

The Burial Ship

Jimmy's wolf died
it wasn't nothing but a cub
O.Z. built a coffin ship
he made it so the head could look out the prow
the river was going to be his grave
we held services there
everyone wore a black mask and we cut ourselves for old
    times' sake
he was laid away
buried in the little ship
there was no sacrifice no dead chickens
we broke a Nugrape bottle over the hull it was full
the ship was about four feet long
Ray Baby and I could have fit in it if we were dead
for sails we stole a tent flap
Six Toes painted it red with a black cross
each one dripped some blood over the wolf in the boat
Melvin said the cold weather set in
we brought the blind child with us to tell the fortunes of
    the future
he always carried a frog gig and wore a top hat

Frank Stanford was born August 1, 1949, in Greenville, Mississippi; he spent his childhood in Greenville and Memphis. He did his schooling at Subiaco Academy in Arkansas and at the University of Arkansas, where he took part in the writing program. He made his home mostly in Northwest Arkansas, where he worked as a land surveyor with his own company and founded Lost Roads Press. He was married to the painter Ginny Stanford. Twelve volumes of his poems have been published, including *The Singing Knives* (1971), *Field Talk* (1975), a 542-page poem called *The Battlefield Where the Moon Says I Love You* (1977), and the posthumous *Crib Death* (1979) and *You* (1979). He produced and directed films on the lives and works of John Crowe Ransom, Richard Eberhart, Richard Wilbur, Malcolm Cowley, and Robert Penn Warren, and was the subject of an impressionistic film by Mill Mountain Studios of Washington. Stanford died by his own hand at his home in Fayetteville, Arkansas, on June 3, 1978.

he reached out his hands and wiggled his fingers
that's the way he knew
he said I need two bits and a little music
he didn't talk right he made it all sound like a song
everyone had dirty white gloves on
we had a jug a guitar and a oil bucket
somebody said woe is the wolf
we thought we heard Mose playing a fife away back in
    the woods
I was on Ace comb and Stage Plank wrapper
Baby Gauge sang Back to the Dust he wailed
I wanted to sing The Blood Done Signed My Name but they
    wouldn't let me
the blind child said he'd have to go to Newport to see
    Aunt Caroline Dye
ashes to ashes dust to dust the devil be had if this old life
    don't get worse
it was getting cold
he said some river rat was liable to use the wolf for bait
better keep watch
the smoke was coming out our mouths
Jimmy wasn't shivering he was just staring at the water
I poked him to see if he was in a trance
he said come on O.Z.
they rowed out to the coffin the ship bearing the dead wolf
they set if afire and watched it burn
there was one big spark that cracked like ash in the dark
it must have been the wolf's eye
it kept on going towards the heavens
it was a shooting star

Called

There was only a penny
on the arm of our phonograph
but it played like like a hundred dollars

Pretty soon we're all going to die
Salamanca was fond of saying
to me as he read the Bible in the outhouse

Now he's got me saying the same
words The moon mosquitoes and darkness
were in his ear
He'd have dreams

A naked white woman washing his feet
The sparrows on his eye

There were only a few chapters
left in the book He listened
to the blues and drank
He sucked ice

He yodelled at old death
when he was wanting some shuteye

Nobody on earth is like me
he'd wake up speaking
just like he was still asleep

Salamanca said he had the sparrows
on his eye
He said I am like the piano
they threw off the bridge
the snakebed and the shadetree
I'm something

He talked to death like a man
fishing in his hole

I'm something not everybody wants
to believe
He'd say sipping on whisky I stole for him

He told death to suck hind teat

Salamanca would kick me out of bed
and holler at me

177 / Frank Stanford

Living with Death

Long ago a man came to our place
With his daughter
It was evening when they arrived
In their wagon

They had a white piano

They asked only to stay the night
For room and board
They said they'd clean the barn

I looked out my window until dawn
Counting the peaches

The maid gave me rags
For the hot pot of coffee
She gave me to take them

I hadn't even milked
Hadn't sung to the fish
But they'd stacked sacks of manure
And sharpened all the tools

So I went to the pump
And found the daughter washing there

She said Death won't dare
Touch a hair on our heads

Allegory of Youth

I suppose that at one time there was a ship
Called Night, named and painted on the bow
In blood by a girl that went by Lucy,
And it had a great cargo, the moon,
As it sailed past all points
East and West of the dark hearts it broke.
On board the blowflies were bad, but the music
Was lovely, like a cat in a wet field.
The sleek ship Night was known for its french afternoons,
Its decks dark as hell and Vermeer, the portholes
Free of horseshit and sad eyes,
The harbors it loved to forget, its duels,
And fantastic library of sin,
The Science of Imaginary Solutions
Written in disappearing ink.
One morning a storm formed, an owl flew
Itself to death around the mast.
Naturally, the ship sank, but all
Was not forgotten, only the warnings.
Ever since, the air's been thick as the dreams
Of migrants polishing their shoes.
And Elmo, the black diver who raised me,
Knows he's getting on in years, knows
What he needs is more sleep,
That he's not long for this world,
But he still has me
Latch down his dark helmet
When he makes the nightly descent.

Conditions Uncertain and Likely

To Pass Away

I went down the road to have supper with Shing. My feet were so pale and warm from the dust when I got there that I pumped water on them, I pumped water over myself, letting it run down over my bare chest and under the belt of my shorts. I stood in the ditch like a wheel. Wearing no drawers, the water went freely down my legs, and the evening wind crawled up under the loose fitting hand-me-down, cut-down pants. I had just come from the Greek's tugboat, and the swarthy and enchanted music he played was still with me, and not even the low wind could make me listen to another thing.

"Did you hear that?" Shing asked me.

"What, where are you?"

"Look and see."

"What was it that you heard?"

"Those womens whispering in the kitchen."

"Where are you?"

"I'm in the tree with the cat. He chased the snake up here."

"I'll help you down; I came to eat with you."

"Yes, it's good that a young man today can remember an old man of yesterday. And how are your teeth? Don't let them go bad like mine. Your mouth is pretty and white, I suppose. You better watch that one, dark tooth. Everything rots."

"Did I......."

"Did I get a letter?"

"Did I leave my book here? No, you didn't. There wasn't anything up at the store."

"Black mail, *stones in my pathway*, are you hungry?"

Shing had lost his sight before he had ever known he was entitled to such a thing. He was born without eyes. A long time ago all they had was two, shining orbs, like ball bearings, and so the Government sent him enough money to buy them. And now it's like looking into bent mirrors. The Government tells him they will buy him new eyes, but he doesn't listen. He likes the old ones. He likes for people to see themselves.

Poor Shing, he was losing his mind like a pond losing water in a dry summer. He said things to you and you knew they weren't true. Like he said he had a son named Woe. He was a ventriloquist and his dummy was named Arimathea. Who would believe that?

Shing had a bad habit of yelling at people when they came by his place. I was afraid they'd come and get him. At church, they took up a special collection to pay the deputy off, just so he'd leave him alone. The only thing he ever did that was real bad was come to the wedding, naked with his white Persian cat. Shing knew the bride when she was a young girl. Everyone thought the ceremony was ruined, all except the bride. She walked back down the aisle, and helped Shing out the door. The priest made an altar boy take off his red cassock and give it to Shing. They heard about it in town, too. The County people heard about it. A man on his tractor said he saw a naked nigger walking down the road with a white rod and a white cat. Some men cutting soap on the porch got the man down off his tractor and hauled him in the beer joint. Everybody was losing their mind and their loves that summer. They were going broke from bad crops, and going crazy from that. Their loving wasn't easy. It was the blood, the blood in Shing's veins, that was doing him in. It was getting hard as okra.

"I know, I know," he said, climbing down the tree, "you're fixing to tell old Shing so long; I know, you got a new buddy, that Greek on the river, and I don't blame you. Maybe you're a little old for Shing now. I see what you're getting at, you're looking at that sawdust falling out of my leg, yea, by God, I know. Well, the mean time is, I'm worse off than Joseph of Arimathea, that dummy, so say so long."

"I'm mighty hungry, Shing."

His big cat was coughing up the feathers hanging from its mouth. A cricket was sitting on the edge of a pail in the corner of his porch, and it wouldn't jump for anything. The wind made the swing creak, so I got a can of Three-In-One Oil and wet the chain where it fastened to the eyes screwed into the ceiling.

He shaved by the window. There was a sock draping his mirror. After so many years the suds from the cakes of soap had filled up the sill like snow. There were some Chinese chimes hanging down from the roof of his porch and when there was no wind he used a fan to blow them together.

"That woman used to come through my yard with that slab of salt pork under her arm. I told that woman. I'd be sitting on the porch, eating sardines and lemons, and I'd hear her open up her polka-dotted parasol . . . ."

There were some dominoes in a wooden box on his table but I never played with him because he cheated. Just because he was blind you figured he wouldn't lose. There were blue bottles from Milk of Magnesia and Vapo-Rub all over. He liked blue. He'd pick the mud dobbers out of their nests and listen to them buzz. He said, "If I had eyes, I wished they'd be blue as dirt dobber wings." People used to set their clocks in their windows at night, but Shing came around and stole them. That summer, while they were losing their love and their fortunes, he lost his mind.

"What will we have?"

"Go get the ladle and taste it."

"Shing, I believe it might be a bad night. A crazy woman might blow in."

"Yes, I can feel the clouds dragging their dead birds. A sister might call."

"I hope not. I'm not mad about the high winds."

"Did you see my letter? I want you to mail it tomorrow."

"God, it's hot out tonight, isn't it Shing?"

"When you bury me, I want a star to be on my rosary. See if anybody will go in on a pyramid. I want a picture by what's his name; one of those high-yellows eating a dew melon. And there's one where she's lying on her belly with a flower in her hair and a black ghost is hiding behind her. I want you to carry all my mahogany outside by the tree, don't let the outhouse smell too much, say it man, and when you wake up take yourself up slow."

I walked into the kitchen.

He called back at me, "It's a beetree in there somewhere, hear it?" "Where the wine at?"

It was hot. I stood up on a bottle case, dipped some of the stew up, and, as I blew on the spoon, my sweat dripped into the black cauldron. The bottle case quivered. I was sweating behind my knees. I went back outside by the man and sat down on the swing. He cooled himself with a fan that came from church. A big eye was drawn on it, right in the center of a pyramid. He was sweating terrible. *Be not forgetful to entertain strangers, for thereby some have seen to angels unawares* was written on the other side of the fan—with HEBREWS 13:1-2.

"It's nice when the sun goes down," I said.

"You bet your boots. It's nice at night. You shut the door, the footsteps die."

"Did you ever find your friend?" I asked him. "No. He must have gotten drunk, and walked off to the woods and died. Ha-ha!"

"He might have stepped off in the quickmud. You know what happened to the catskinner?"

"They never found the bulldozer. They let down the anchors in the earth and never touched anything. Nothing was certain. The mud is too deep. Deeper than my mother's lamp. I carried it for the ghosts in the hollow. Where's that baseball? Down in the bushes? You can't fool Shing. And here I come like a shadow. You think I'm looking where I'm going? It ain't likely. Ain't old Shing a sight?"

"I was hoping you'd tell me a story before supper, Shing."

"You betrayed me. I'm scared and lonely. Ha-ha. Get the Greek to coo. Ha-ha."

"What about one for old time's sake?"

"Shit. I was hoping you'd tell me who's been stealing the cornbread off my backporch."

"No one, Shing."

"It's them womens."

"Maybe an animal?"

"Ha-ha. Fool. Animal don't leave wrappers. Don't leave. Don't smell like rancid butter. Animal know when a gut's too gone I won't mention it. Thank you. Don't mention it. Goddamn, there was a moon and her hair was like wheat."

"Somebody brings their own butter, then steals your bread. Now that is what I call a story."

"A dog wouldn't smell like that. No boy, that is the truth. I got to quick calling you that. You want to play some bones later? Is the ladder still up side the beetree, is there a clean room for the visitors?"

We ate hot food for such a warm night. The wind blew the dust in our eyes.

"Don't see how the Mexicans do it," I told him.

He drank a bottle of Tabasco and started hollering. He hollered from way down deep in his guts, like he had cancer. I had to drink four Nehi's. I was opening a fifth one, but chipped the neck off the bottle. Shing said not to drink it. He said there was liable to be more glass in the bottle. He had me strain it through a minnow sieve. He didn't know a small piece of glass could even get through that. I knew there was a piece of glass in it, but I drank it anyway. I shut my eyes and took a long swallow. He never stopped yelling. Someone heard him, and stopped in on us to call. They were strangers.

Some other people stopped. They were strangers, too. They left.

There were many people on the road. They knew something was coming, so they were travelling. Shing quit hollering. Then he started laughing. Then he grabbed me by the neck.

"Sometimes," he said, "you can stop dead in your tracks and hear your footsteps go on."

A wagon came by, the white dust splashing through the spokes of the wheels like flour through a woman's hands. Shing put the broken bottle neck on his finger.

"Is there two people in that rig?"

"There are," I said.

"Is one tall and the other short?"

"Yes."

"That'd be my son Woe, and his dummy, Joseph of Arimathea."

**Carl Judson Launius**

October Song Ad Adagio

The first Ozark frosts set fire to the hills.
The stands of maple, gum, and sycamore
inflame the hollows, rise up to color
the near ridges in masquerade of Hell's
Uplands. Here, in this pyre of a spent year,
a stark image of fire consumes my mind:
a quick rage that dazzles, then fades in the wind,
leaving stripped limbs askance in winter air.

What could I hope for that this season, turning,
might find I'd made a difference? I don't know.
I don't know. I watch the first leaves falling:
how they drift about at the wind's whim, their slow
journey to ultimate blank walls, there forming
motleys that grow first rusty, then white with snow.

Carl Judson Launius was born in Poplar Bluff, Missouri, August 21, 1946. He moved with his family to Corning, Arkansas, where a high school football injury left him paralyzed from the neck down. He graduated from the University of Illinois in 1972 with a B. A. in English and took an M. F. A. in poetry from the University of Arkansas in 1978. His first volume of poems, *Neutral-Tinted Haps*, was published on his birthday (by coincidence) in 1980. He lives now in Hot Springs, where he is resident poet to the Arkansas Rehabilitation Center.

One Night Frank Stanford Got Drunk,

And Started Humming an

Old-Timey Spiritual

When you're at the Safeway doing the week's shopping,
Death is in the Produce Section, thumping the melons.
When you're at Roger's Pool Hall, chalking up a snooker cue,
Death is sipping a Pabst, watching the Evening News.
You often come up behind Death on a hill or a curve.
He has a '51 Ford pickup that holds a steady 40 miles an hour.
When you're at home in bed with your lover,
Death is in your closet trying on your 3-piece suits.
Coats and shirts never fit him because his arms are extra long.
They have to be, for scattering poisons on internal organs;
for tripping great-grandmothers at the tops of stairs;
for tipping over piroques carrying duck hunters up the river;
for nudging airplanes off radar scanners;
for squishing fetuses, and stopping old hearts in their sleep.
Death can reach as deep as the bottom of a coal shaft,
as high as the Golden Gate Bridge.

Sometimes Death is a woman. You meet her in a bar
and pick up the tab. She really holds her liquor well.
You try to take her home, but you're too drunk to see the road.
She drives. She floors the accelerator on the highway.
She takes aim at oncoming headlights.
She walks away from the wreckage without a scratch.
The Highway Patrol reports no witnesses.

Death is a moody sort.
He can be discreet as a mortician.
He can be precise and efficient, like a German scientist.
He can be rough and crude, even mean,
like an NFL linebacker, or an Arizona sheriff's deputy.

His sense of timing could be described as whimsical.

You might be getting stoned to Rahsaan Kirk's *The Inflatable
    Tear,*

or going to a Laurel & Hardy Film Festival,
or watching the Celtics play the Knicks at the Boston Garden,
or viewing the New York skyline from the Staten Island Ferry,
or playing softball in the park on an Indian Summer afternoon,
or checking the air in your tires at the Gulf station,
or bending over to tie a shoe....

You look up, and there's Death standing in front of you.
He says *Well Hot Damn* and slaps your shoulder.
He wants to become better acquainted.
He doesn't necessarily want to be friends.

He Watches Arkansas Whip Southern Cal

And Recalls Old Football Injuries

Even sitting in the cramped wheelchair section
I could see the AstroTurf bristling. The stands
were livid with Arkansas red, rooters yelling
PIG SOOIEE! hard into the night wind.
Down on the field were some of the biggest sons
of bitches I'd thought possible entrenched along
the scrimmage line, and flashy backs who could run
over tacklers, or leave defenders standing.
At the final gun, we all jumped up and screamed.

Or for a flying second I thought I did,
so inflamed I was. And with all the size and speed
gathered on that field, not a single damned soul
popped a harder lick than the one I laid
on a running back in my last highschool game.
His teammates had to help him back to his bench,
and there, fighting the pain, he fell to his knees
and broke down, gagging into fallen leaves
while I lay waiting for the ambulance.

 **Lynn Graznak**

Growing Up in Bongo Congo

We are the cartoon generation,
from when Truman fired Howdy Doody.
      We are conditioned to be tolerantly amused,
      seeing Spiro Agnew as Bosco Bear.
We are willing to accept
a Kellogg's Variety Pak of realities.
Most of us knew Yogi Bear better
than we knew our own fathers.
Captain Kangaroo spent more time with us.
        The end of the world will come to us
        as a sort of Disneyland program
        drawn by Hieronymus Bosch.
  Three fingered mice in tuxedoes
  will dance across the screen,
  before our president,
  dressed as Clarabelle Clown
  comes out with that last
  seltzer bottle.

Lynn Graznak was born May 8, 1949, in Canton, Ohio, and raised in Missouri, where she has spent most of her life. She makes her home in Columbia, where she is working toward a degree in graphic design at Stephens College, writes poems and stories, studies the roles of woman in mythology, and raises Egyptian Mau cats.

Acknowledgments

"A Joyous River" and "Utopia in Arkansas," by Charles J. Finger, reprinted from *Ozark Fantasia* (Golden Horseman Press, 1927), reprinted with the permission of Helen F. Leflar.

"Our Home Back Yonder," by Wayman Hogue, reprinted from *Back Yonder: An Ozark Chronicle* (Mentor, 1932). Reprinted with permission of the literary executors of Charlie May Fletcher.

"America's Yesterday," by Thomas Hart Benton, reprinted from *An Ozark Anthology* (Caxton, 1940), edited by Vance Randolph.

"I Arrive in the Hill Country," by Otto Ernest Rayburn, reprinted from *Forty Years in the Ozarks* (Ozark Guide Press, 1957).

"Verbal Modesty in the Ozarks," reprinted from *Dialect Notes* 5. "Literary Words in the Ozarks," reprinted from *American Speech* 4 and *An Ozark Anthology* (Caxton Printers, 1940). "A Good Song Well Sang," reprinted from *From an Ozark Holler* (Vanguard, 1933). All three works by Vance Randolph, reprinted with the permission of Mary P. Randolph.

"The New Calf," "Setting a Spell," "Omens," and "Remedies," by Fred Starr, reprinted from *Pebbles from the Ozarks* (Bar D Press, 1942).

"Four Seasons at Possum Trot Farm," by Leonard Hall, originally appeared as "Sumacs Blazing and Geese Flying Low," "Chopping Wood," "Signs of Spring," and "Summer's Flowers Begin to Bloom," in *Possum Trot Farm: An Ozark Journal* (Caledonia Press, 1949).

"Winter Moon," "Dream Variations," and "Cross," by Langston Hughes, copyright 1926 by Alfred A. Knopf, Inc., and renewed 1954 by Langston Hughes. Reprinted from *Selected Poems*, by Langston Hughes, by permission of Alfred A. Knopf, Inc.

"The Bloody Brothers," by Robert L. Morris, reprinted from *An Ozark Anthology* (Caxton, 1940), edited by Vance Randolph.

"Notes for a Prayer to Be Recalled at Thanksgiving," by Ward Allison Dorrance, reprinted from *We're from Missouri* (Missourian Press, 1938).

"Ribbon," by Don West, reprinted from *Broadside to the Sun* (W. W. Norton, 1946).

"Windy Spears," by Francis Irby Gwaltney, reprinted from *Idols and Axel Grease* (Bobbs-Merrill, 1974).

"About Grampa, Who Died Poor," by Edsel Ford, reprinted from *Looking for Shiloh* (University of Missouri Press, 1968).

"An Ozark Gardener, 86, Awaits Coming of the Greening Season," "Cats, Cattle, and People—Beware of Dog Days," by Roy Reed. © 1975/76 by The New York Times Company. Reprinted by permission.

"The Wall," by Miller Williams, reprinted from *Shenandoah* 16, 3 (Spring 1965).

"Down the Blue Hole," by William Harrison, reprinted from *Roller Ball Murder* (Morrow, 1974).

"The Current Revisited," by Harry Minetree, reprinted from *Sports Afield* (April 1978).

"The Travelling Picker's Prayer and Dream," "Having Gained Some Spiritual Ruthlessness But Still Confused by What Has Happened, A Local Man Considers A Friend Who Died Alone," "The Country Music Star Begins His Politics," "Dealing with Mary Fletcher," by James Whitehead, reprinted from *Local Men* (University of Illinois Press, 1979).

"Poems on the I Ching," by Robert Dyer, reprinted from *Oracle of the Turtle* (Singing Wind Press, 1979). Reprinted by permission of the author and Singing Wind Press.

"Poem about a Farm Boy Who Went to College and Returned to the Farm," by John Stoss, reprinted from *Finding the Broom* (Lost Roads Press). Reprinted by permission of Lost Roads Press.

"This Entangled Season," by Eugene Warren, reprinted from the *Ozark Review* (Summer 1979).

"Blackberries," "Apology for Hope," by Jack Butler, reprinted from *West of Hollywood* (August House Publishing Cooperative, 1980).

"Let Her Travel Far," by Paul Johnson, reprinted from *Boon County Fare*, ed. by Karlene Gentile (Singing Wind Press, 1975). Reprinted by permission of Singing Wind Press.

"To All Those Considering Coming to Fayetteville." In *Often Different Landscapes*. Copyright © 1976 by Leon Stokesbury. Reprinted by permission of the publisher, The University of Texas Press. "Sometimes," by Leon Stokesbury, reprinted from *The Drifting Away of All We Once Held Essential* (Trilobite, 1979).

"The Bad Cat," by Speer Morgan, reprinted from *Frog Gig and Other Stories* (University of Missouri Press, 1976).

"Leaf Stone and Wind," by Karlene Gentile, reprinted from *Boone County Fare*, ed. by Karlene Gentile (Singing Wind Press, 1975). Reprinted by permission of Singing Wind Press.

"The New Savage," by John Looney, reprinted from *Headwaters* (August House Publishing Cooperative, 1979).

"Meta, Mo.," by Walter Bargen, reprinted from *Fields of Thenar* (Singing Wind Press, 1980).

"Obedience of the Corpse," reprinted from *Terrorism* (Lost Roads Press). "Room Rented by a Single Woman in Van Buren, Arkansas," reprinted from *Room Rented by a Single Woman* (Lost Roads Press). Both works by C. D. Wright. Reprinted by permission of Lost Roads Press.

"The Burial Ship," "Allegory of Youth," reprinted from *You* (Lost Roads Press). Reprinted by permission of Lost Roads Press. "Called," "Living with Death," reprinted from *Shade* (Mill Mountain Press, 1975). Reprinted by permission of C. D. Wright. "Conditions Uncertain and Likely to Pass Away," reprinted from *Grapevine* (December 10, 1975). Reprinted by permission of Lost Roads Press. All five works by Frank Stanford.

"October Song ad Adagio," "One Night Frank Stanford Got Drunk and Started Humming an Old-Timey Spiritual," "He Watches Arkansas Whip

Southern Cal, and Recalls Old Football Injuries," by Carl Judson Launius, reprinted from *Neutral-Tinted Haps* (Veiled Horn Press, 1980). Reprinted by permission of Veiled Horn Press.

"Growing Up in Bongo Congo," by Lynn Graznak, reprinted from *Boone County Fare*, ed. by Karlene Gentile (Singing Wind Press, 1975). Reprinted by permission of Singing Wind Press.